extreme sail

Oliver Dewar

FOREWORD BY DAME ELLEN MACARTHUR

PAVILION

CONTENTS

Foreword

To me sailing is a passion: an intoxicating ride along a path that is totally unpredictable, wild and powerful. But the sea needs to be respected. It has the ability to make you seem like the smallest object on the planet; it can toss you over with a flick of a wave and it has no compassion for its actions. It is this excitement that fuels my dedication to the sport of sailing.

At four years old I stepped on a boat with my aunt — it was to be a life changing experience. I loved the freedom of being out on the water; it was a totally new and exhilarating feeling. Of course, the more I learnt, the more my appetite for the challenge of the water grew, and by the time I was 18, sailing around Britain on my own in my 21ft boat *Iduna* — my fate was sealed. I continued to push the boundaries with each new project and sailing in the Mini Transat solo transatlantic race in 1997 led to the dream of the Vendée Globe — a legendary race that makes heroes of some sailors while claiming the lives of others. Twenty years after setting foot on a boat for the first time, I found myself in *Les Sables d'Olonne* preparing for the biggest race of my life so far. For

title page *A new perspective for world water-ski champion Patrice Martin behind Yvan Bourgnon's 60ft trimaran,* Rexona.

below *Ellen MacArthur takes a digital self-portrait with a companion during her record-breaking solo circumnavigation in 2004–5. MacArthur and trimaran B&Q were blasted by freezing hail at 51° South in the Pacific Ocean.*

4

most, the Vendèe Globe is the ultimate race in single-handed sailing – it pushes sailors to their very limits, mentally and physically, and tests every skill they have on the water. But as the saying goes, "to win, first you have to finish" and this is never more true than in this race. After 94 days at sea, I returned back to the same port that *Kingfisher* and I slipped away from in November 2000, having given everything to this race. It had been a roller-coaster ride but on the inside, I was still 'the same Ellen' – the girl with boundless enthusiasm for the sea and everything it has to offer.

After nearly ten years of professional sailing I continue to be grateful for the opportunities this sport has given me. In every race and every record attempt, I am given the opportunity to do better: to learn more and gain more understanding of this great sport and the environment to which it belongs. In my eyes, the Southern Ocean is one of the most beautiful environments on the planet. During the round-the-world record attempt on board the trimaran *B&Q*, I witnessed some incredible storms and, while at times I was concerned about how we would get through, I was also in awe at the beauty and power of the sea around me – sometimes dealing with the storm you are in is easier than the preparation and waiting in anticipation! As sailors we are privileged to be able to experience these oceans – the rawness and intensity – that have been shared by so few; more people have reached the summit of Everest than have raced non-stop around the world!

Sailing is a fantastic challenge; whether racing or cruising, there are many elements beyond our control, which bring a unique excitement and satisfaction. Although I have raced in many events, both fully crewed and solo, nothing is achieved without a real team effort. For me – and, I think for many who sail – to feel like an integral part of the crew or team; to work together getting to the finish line or getting through a storm brings the greatest sense of satisfaction.

Ultimately, the sea is my home – it is where I feel most content. I know that sailing is a passion that many people all over the world share. It is that passion and enjoyment that takes us out on to the sea. This book opens up that world, taking a look at all the major yachting events around the globe: from inshore to offshore, from solo to crewed – all illustrated by a collection of stunning photos.

I hope you enjoy this book – may it go with you wherever you sail!

Ellen MacArthur

Dame Ellen MacArthur MBE
Skipper trimaran *B&Q*
www.ellenmacarthur.com

Ocean, n. A body of water occupying about two-thirds of a world made for man – who has no gills.

Ambrose Bierce (1842–c.1914),
The Devil's Dictionary

Introduction

It can be argued that setting out to sea in any vessel before accurate navigation methods evolved in the mid-1700s was extreme and to be avoided. For many, this logic holds true today, regardless of advances in boat design, technology and onboard communication systems. But what drives some men to venture into the remote, watery deserts of the planet? Any attempt to answer this question requires a brief study of man's history afloat.

Early offshore sailing was stimulated exclusively by trade and settlement, beginning with the Greek and Roman expeditions to India and China during the Hellenistic period (323–31 BC), and continuing, at around the time of Christ's birth, with Polynesian rafts filtering east across the Pacific Ocean, reaching Easter Island and Hawaii sometime between AD300–400. In about the year AD1,000, Norse sailors left Europe, calling into Iceland before briefly settling in North America, while during the thirteenth and fourteenth centuries, Marco Polo sailed throughout Asia and Ibn Battuta visited the Islamic countries of Africa, Europe and the Far East. By the early fifteenth century, fleets of Chinese junks were regularly crossing the Indian Ocean returning home with exotic treasures and curiosities for Emperor Ming. As navigation, chart making and shipbuilding practices improved, sailors travelled over increasing distances.

The true size of the planet and oceans, however, remained a mystery until the Golden Age of Exploration in the late fifteenth and sixteenth centuries. Christopher Columbus crossed the mid-Atlantic in 1492 (500 years after Leif Eriksson crossed the northern Atlantic), 'discovering' the New World and igniting an intense era of trans-oceanic sailing; Portuguese ships streamed south along the dark, mysterious coast of Africa and around the Cape of Good Hope into the Indian Ocean. Meanwhile, Spanish expeditions headed west into the Atlantic, then down the coast of South America and into the Pacific: both nations dispatching sailors to dangerous, diseased, uncharted areas of the globe in the name of god, glory and gold.

Since the fleet led by Ferdinand Magellan (c.1480–1521) first circumnavigated the globe, sailors have continued to risk their lives at sea, although in more recent times, some have done so without the desire to colonize, convert or pillage remote areas of the planet. In 1968, Sir Robin Knox-Johnston completed the first single-handed, non-stop circumnavigation of the globe. In the log of this journey he claimed (during a brief bout of introspection), "I was sailing around the world simply because I bloody well wanted to – and, I realized, I was thoroughly enjoying myself." Conversely, Knox-Johnston's

6

Surely oak and threefold brass surrounded his heart who first trusted a frail vessel to the merciless ocean?

Horace (65–8 BC), Roman poet

Prima ego veliuolis ambiui Cursibus Orbem
Magellane nouo te duce ducta freto.
Ambiui. meritoq̃ vocor VICTORIA: sunt mî
Vela, alæ, preciũ, gloria, pugna, mare.

FERDINA MAGELLAN · 15 20.

Paragones: Magelanici Fretum
Terra de fogo.
15 77.

FRANCISCVS DRACO

SEBAST. DE CANO · 15 21.

Primus me circumdedisti Magellani 16 01.

OLIVIER ANORT VLTRAIEC

· VICTORIA ·

Conueniunt rebus nomina sepe suis.

No. — THE FIRST SHIP TO CIRCUMNAVIGATE THE WORLD.

7

direct contemporary, the legendary French circumnavigator, Bernard Moitessier (1925–1994), suggested a more spiritual and poetic spur for wandering the oceans, saying: "You do not ask a tame seagull why he needs to disappear from time to time towards the open sea. He goes, that's all."

Whatever inspires men to sail beyond the limit of normal human endurance, a diverse cultural legacy remains: for many Anglo-Saxon sailors the sea represents a challenge to be endured and conquered, yet for their French counterparts, the sea is often considered a supreme, primeval force of nature connecting man with his soul. One of the aims of *Extreme Sail* is to reveal the environment that has generated this range of conviction.

Furthermore, this book aims to unite the various modern disciplines within the sport: inshore and offshore, big boats and dinghies, cruising and racing. Although many insist that the sea binds together all levels and sectors of the sport in a salty, marine brotherhood, this belief is misguided. Many inshore racing crews regard offshore sailors as courageous Neanderthals, while these ocean-racing primates view their shore-based relatives as delicate, coastal flowers. Many cruising

above *A representation of Ferdinand Magellan and his ship,* Victoria, *during the world's first circumnavigation, 1519–1522.*

yachtsmen consider racing crews to be arrogant speed freaks who, in return, often treat cruisers as mossy-bottomed obstacles cluttering a race course (in reality, the only consensus among sailors is the belief that large motor yachts should be treated with contempt). *Extreme Sail* attempts to demolish the maze of partitions that exist within the sport.

Finally, the images in *Extreme Sail* aim to find a thread of common, seafaring purpose – to establish a link between the mutinous, superstitious pioneers of Magellan's voyage and modern sailors on their racing thoroughbreds bristling with satellite technology.

above *Sir Robin Knox-Johnston approaches the end of the first non-stop single-handed voyage around the world in his 32ft ketch,* Suhaili, *after 313 days at sea.* Suhaili *averaged 4.04 knots during the 30,123-mile circumnavigation. Note that the self-steering system at the stern has been destroyed.*

right *Technology has changed the character of the sport, but not the nature of the ocean or man's endurance. Australian skipper Nick Moloney puts Open 60,* Skandia, *to the test in the run-up to the 2004–5 Vendée Globe.*

skandia:
Gartmore
Merrill Lynch
Investment Managers
INVESCO PERPETUAL
vendéeglobe
Sodebo
skandia
skandia:

1

Inshore

- WHAT'S IT ALL ABOUT?

- THE RULES AND WHAT
  TO DO WITH THEM

- IN THE BEGINNING…

What's it all about?

There are two distinct styles of inshore sailing: you can cruise, or you can race. Cruising generally involves leaving Point A and arriving at the desired destination, Point B, ahead of a fixed deadline, such as high or low water, lunchtime, a pre-arranged cocktail hour, before the supermarket closes or before onboard relationships break down irretrievably. Between Points A and B, a yacht's skipper and crew must negotiate the natural variables of wind, tide, depth and current and remain aware of any man-made hazards; other sailing yachts, commercial shipping, submerged wrecks or structures, and motorboats. Whether you are cruising off Martha's Vineyard or the Galapagos Islands, these basic principles apply.

Inshore racing, however, involves leaving Point A at precisely the same time as a number of other yachts, then visiting Points B, C, D, E and F before arriving at Point G. Reaching the destination and finishing a race safely is crucial, but to do this quickly and ahead of any other yachts is a fundamentally important goal. Achieving this objective successfully requires years of practice and experience and can absorb huge sums of money. This sector of sailing, though, is a unique arena where racing novices can compete alongside, or against, professionals; America's Cup grandees and Olympic legends may find themselves approaching a racing mark at the same time as an inexperienced weekend sailor whose grasp of the Racing Rules of Sailing is minimal. Although these circumstances can prove stressful and, occasionally, expensive, they are unrivalled in sport and add colour and excitement to every inshore race or regatta.

The global appeal and diversity of inshore racing is vast. On any given stretch of coastline anywhere in the world, evidence of competitive sailing is usually to be found. This can range from off-duty fishermen in East Africa to financial analysts enjoying a corporate hospitality regatta

12

Though no scientific corollary has yet been published, sailors, as people, tend to be frighteningly Jekyll-and-Hyde-like. Some of the nicest guys on land can be the meanest !&*?s on the water

Dave Perry, yachtsman and author (from *Winning In One-Designs*)

previous page *Designed for solo or two-handed offshore marathons, Orma 60 trimarans provide a surreal spectacle when fully crewed and powered-up for inshore races.*

left *Corinthian sailing at its most extreme – rounding Gurnard Ledge buoy west of Cowes. X One-Designs have been competing on the Solent for nearly 100 years and with seventy-nine entries the class provided the biggest racing fleet at Skandia Cowes Week 2005.*

in European waters: polar opposites, culturally, but connected by sport. The annual New Year's Day dhow race circumnavigating the island of Lamu off Kenya is raced in boats that have changed little in design over the past 500 years, while the world's biggest regatta, Skandia Cowes Week, held every August off the southern coast of England, attracted over 1,000 entries in 2005. Although the eight days of racing at Cowes Week are a high-profile showcase for the latest innovations, the intent, approach and competitive atmosphere is identical to the mariners of the Kenyan coastline. Strategy, technique and testosterone dominate both events and post-race debriefings are indistinguishable; eavesdrop on a conversation over mango juice in Lamu after a dhow race and the themes will be interchangeable with a beer-tent debate in Cowes. Interestingly, there is one onshore habit – a language, even – that is common to yacht racers globally, known as 'Karate Sailing'; an activity involving the use of hand-chopping movements to illustrate the tacks and gybes of opposing boats and which often involves using an empty bottle as a windward mark.

At Cowes Week, start line infringements are recorded on CCTV and computer software assists in setting individual courses for the forty different classes, but technological arrogance is inappropriate. It should be noted that the largest and most fiercely competitive racing class during Britain's premier regatta is the ancient X One-Design (XOD) first produced in 1909; seventy-nine of these 20ft keelboats raced in 2005 and these heavy, wooden vessels are wetter and slower than any craft of Lamu.

above *A momentary loss of concentration can turn a day out racing into a whole new world of pain.* Carabistouille *receives a Cowes Week reminder that inshore racing is not always plain sailing.*

next page *The extreme glamour of the Costa Smeralda adds to the attraction of big boat racing at regattas based in Porto Cervo, Sardinia.*

You haven't won the race, if in winning the race you've lost the respect of your competition

Paul Elvström, Danish yachtsman and

winner of four Olympic sailing gold medals

The rules and what to do with them

For many sailors, yacht racing represents temporary freedom from shore-based routine set in a fiercely competitive environment. It is, therefore, essential that the sport be governed by a set of rules. The use and application of these laws reveal two distinct species of racing yachtsman: those who will race within the rules and use their knowledge and skill to win through tactical excellence, and those who will occasionally attempt to race outside the rules. The choice of flouting the racing rules may be driven by a number of factors; the high stakes of prestige, publicity, money and ego can all contribute to this decision. It would be inappropriate in *Extreme Sail* to explain the rules in any depth, but a brief glance at the most important aspects will assist in understanding the appeal and emotional intensity of inshore racing.

There are essentially two types of sailing rules within the Racing Rules of Sailing (RRS): the 'technical' rules and 'human' rules. Both varieties are vital to racing and are frequently revised by the International Sailing Federation (ISAF) to keep pace with a sport that is constantly developing. In addition, a yacht will be subject to class rules, which apply to everyone racing a particular type of boat, and 'Sailing Instructions', which apply to every competitor in each individual race series or regatta.

The overall aims of the RRS are to promote safety, equality and sportsmanship in yacht racing and ensure that any person or yacht infringing these rules should receive a penalty. The 'technical' rules govern all the variables that can arise when boats are racing: rights of way, propulsion methods and the complex definitions employed in competitive sailing. 'Human' rules offer directions on conduct and behaviour when racing, including the recent introduction of anti-doping laws. From 100ft maxi yachts competing offshore in the Mediterranean to radio-controlled model boats racing on small, urban ponds – these rules apply equally to every racing yacht from the moment the preparatory signal for her race has been made. Any punishment for an infringement is either carried out during the race, when the offending yacht undertakes an immediate, pre-arranged penalty manoeuvre, or in front of an independent protest committee provided by the race organisation. In the latter case, a jury of racing experts will make a judgement if any protest is contested (i.e. the alleged offender denies breaking the rules) or a yacht fails to take a penalty manoeuvre while racing.

Possibly the most fundamental 'technical' rule involves 'overlap': a right-of-way and overtaking principle that causes more debate than all the other rules within the RRS combined. Another heavily argued point is Rule 42 (RRS 2005–2008), which is concerned with 'propulsion'

opposite *Race leaders bunch together in a gybing match downwind off St Tropez during the Dragon class 75th anniversary regatta in 2005.*

above *Onboard blood pressures rise as views on overlap and right of way are exchanged between IRC boats at the Spi Ouest regatta 2005.*

above *Race yacht or circus act? A Dragonfly's nimble crew rearrange their complex multi-trapeze system during the Centomiglia on Lake Garda, Italy.*

and the use of illegal and repetitive actions by the crew to assist the movement of a yacht racing in light winds. The rule includes guidelines on such exotic tricks as 'fanning', 'flicking', 'pumping' and 'torquing' and what a crew should do if they suspect an opposing boat of entering the mysterious 'yellow light area' (an occasion when a yacht's crew may be on the verge of repeating a dubious and potentially illegal motion). Rule 42.2(c) goes even further and prohibits the activity of 'ooching': this involves one or more of the crew running from the aft end of a becalmed boat, then abruptly halting near the bow and, thereby illegally propelling the yacht forwards. To anyone unfamiliar with yacht racing these examples from the RRS illustrate both the lengths to which sailors will go to win races and the importance of understanding the complex language and definitions in the sport.

The 'human' rules, however, are more understandable – superficially. Rule 2 of the RRS concerns 'Fair Sailing' and requires that yachts and their crews "shall compete in compliance with recognized principles of sportsmanship and fair play." This rule relies on a sailor's personal integrity and a traditional interpretation of Rule 2 prohibits intimidation on the racecourse. For example, the skipper of a yacht with no right of way (on port tack) may begin dishonestly yelling

"Starboard!" at a yacht who has the right of way (on starboard tack) and who is under no obligation to alter her course to avoid the approaching yacht and her screaming helmsman. Due to inexperience, panic, inexpert knowledge of the rules or purely wishing to avoid being rammed, the innocent yacht may throw itself into a manoeuvre away from the potential danger zone and lose valuable ground. Some sailors will regard this action as the height of gamesmanship and a valid necessity born of competition – part of the psychological struggle between sportsmen. This intentional misuse of a right-of-way rule, though, transcends ideas of "sportsmanship and fairplay" and may result in the transgressor being penalised under Rule 69 'Allegations of Gross Misconduct'. Section 69.2(a) of the rule states that a race authority may act and punish a yachtsman upon hearing "a report alleging conduct that has brought the sport into disrepute." This noble sentiment is intrinsic to sportsmanship and the purity of the sport, but may be invoked as an effective way of silencing any embarrassing, awkward criticism of a competitor, a race organisation or a racing authority and is open to misuse.

below *Some obsessive-compulsive behaviour is allowed within the Racing Rules of Sailing (RRS). A Spi Ouest regatta crew attempt to reduce waterline drag with some last minute housework shortly before the start gun.*

In the beginning…

So, how did this variation and complexity start? The roots of inshore yacht racing are found in the town of Cowes on the northern tip of the Isle of Wight, just two miles off the southern coast of England. Here, on a narrow stretch of water called the Solent, the sport was established as an exclusive and fashionable pastime of the very rich. Self-regulated by membership-only yacht clubs and dominated by the Royal Yacht Squadron (RYS), yacht racing languished in a gentle atmosphere of carefully manicured club lawns and revolved around bonnets, baronets and black tie balls. A popular misconception surrounding Cowes is the belief that the magnificent yachts of the late nineteenth century, and their owners were entirely responsible for popularising the sport. Certainly, paintings and photographs of these elegant craft powering along under clouds of canvas are evocative and enduring. This supremely confident period is typified by the 1893 tussle between *Britannia*, belonging to the Prince of Wales and launched the previous year, and the American yacht *Ivanhoe*. In one particular race, the British yacht clutched victory on the final beat, defeating her faster nemesis and prompting the era's senior yachting journalist, Brook Heckstall-Smith, to comment: "*Britannia* had beaten her [*Ivanhoe*] to windward, and somehow or other we never had any fear of an American sloop in British waters again…" (clearly the loss of the America's Cup forty-two years earlier had left a deep scar).

At the time, such admiration was not unanimous. Professor Sir Walter Alexander Raleigh (1861–1922), a direct descendant of Britain's swashbuckling, codpiece-clad hero, bristled: "The so-called yachtsmen of Cowes, it seems, have champagne lunches in the Solent, and then spread canvas and take two hours' run when the breeze is fair and light… They meet the same people at Cowes as they meet later at grouse … different clothes and the same well-fed, carefully exercised bodies, the same bored minds tired of wondering whether passion will ever come their way."

Although Raleigh had a point, the situation was rapidly changing. For while the membership portcullis at the RYS was raised only to admit those with the bluest blood or biggest wallet, the less high born were busy in half decked boats crewed by two or three people, such as the 1-Rater, ½-Rater and 2½-Rater classes. Through the proliferation of these smaller boats, the Solent claimed its early status as a centre for sailing and, soon, affordable yacht racing spread to America and the Continent. This period, the 1880s and 1890s, produced a shrewd anecdote that still has resonance:

Big boat professional skipper: "Would you care to take the helm, Sir?"
Big boat owner: "Thanks, Captain, but I take nothing between meals."

above *Represented racing up the Solent towards Cowes in 1893,* Britannia *epitomizes an era of massive sailing yachts and their noble owners. During a sailing career spanning forty-three years, the yacht competed in 635 races, winning 231 and taking second and third in 129.*

In 1936, after the death of her final owner, George V, Britannia *was towed into deep water off the southern tip of the Isle of Wight and scuttled in accordance with the late king's wishes.*

The most tangible evidence of this period is to catch a glimpse of the huge classic yachts that still compete in inshore races around the world. Partially restored or totally rebuilt, they recall an era of elitism and private financial commitment to yacht racing that is unmatched today. The passion for these marine masterpieces, though, remains unchanged and while the racing may be more sedate in terms of speed than modern yachts, the competitive rivalry at classic regattas is fanatical; these yachts are far more than expensive, attractive toys for self-indulgent millionaires.

The Royal Yacht Squadron: The hardest club in the world to get into or away from. Ladies who are permitted to enter the RYS grounds are required to speak quietly and to wear stockings, though it is hard to believe that a Member of the Squadron would ever look with sufficient interest at a lady's legs to see whether she was wearing stockings or not.

From a glossary of technical sailing terms by Patrick Boyle, c.1938

left *A crewman is sent aloft on* Adix *during the Voiles des St Tropez regatta in the South of France. A great part of the expense in classic yachting is paying for a competent and acrobatic crew.*

right *Built in 1933,* Velsheda *required thirty crew for racing. Rescued from a mud berth in southern England in 1984, she now appears at many classic regattas around the world and won all three races in the 'Spirit of Tradition Class A' at Antigua Classic Week 2005.*

2

The America's Cup Challenge

- A SPORT ON ITS OWN

- WHY, WHEN AND
WHO'S WHO?

- THINGS TO DO ON AN
AMERICA'S CUP YACHT

- HOW TO WIN

A sport on its own

There is little point attempting to combine the America's Cup Challenge (ACC) with any other division of sailing; the event stands alone and the personalities, the racing environment, the boats and the objectives of the competitors are unique. Through intense media coverage, the ACC is the most publicly accessible sailing event on earth, but it is also one of the most misunderstood arenas of yachting. Detractors will claim that the ACC is little more than a handful of multi-millionaires and their over-paid teams indulging in a private regatta. Indeed, the event's long and often controversial history continues to astonish ACC enthusiasts and this, coupled with the immense amounts of money and subsequent glamour this naturally generates, will always attract criticism. However, even the most cynical observer must concede that the America's Cup is never dull.

In 1992 the Kansas billionaire, Bill Koch, took over the role of defending the ACC from foreign raiders and keeping the cup on American soil. Koch is attributed with commenting: "The America's Cup is a race of management, money, technology, teamwork and – last and incidentally – sailing"; a memorable soundbite that quickly become a rallying cry for yachting purists. The truth, however, is far more complex. The ACC is about passion and this manifests itself in a number of forms: competitiveness, skill, ego, avarice and devotion – essentially, all the components and emotions that exist in yachting, but to an extreme degree.

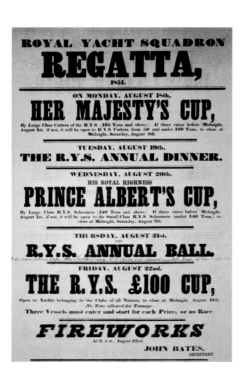

left *British yachtsmen were reluctant to race a mysterious challenger from America until press accusations of cowardice forced a contest. Consequently, the '100 Sovereigns Cup', inexplicably changed by the victors to the '100 Guinea Cup', disappeared to America and the world's greatest yacht racing challenge was born.*

above, right *Almost half the crew of* K-Challenge *crowd the foredeck for a spinnaker* drop in Marseilles during the opening Louis Vuitton Act of the 2007 America's Cup.

previous page *The best view in the house during a fleet race in Valencia. A 'windseeker' will be sent aloft in light airs to identify areas of breeze on the racecourse by spotting bands of ripples or wavelets on the water's surface.*

The America's Cup is the most important sailing competition and one of the most famous sporting events in the world. In sport, there will always be a winner and a loser. That's where the beauty of it resides.

Biotech millionaire, Ernesto Bertarelli, shortly after winning the
America's Cup Challenge in 2003 with *Alinghi*

Why, when and who's who?

A quick study of the challenge's history since the Cup's inception in 1851 is necessary to fully grasp why the ACC is a legendary event and how its modern format has evolved. Knowledge of the historical and contemporary personalities involved will help explain why the names of many ACC heroes and villains are spoken in soft tones of respect, or never mentioned at all. Finally, the following timeline may help a spectator forgive – or at least comprehend – the ACC some of its litigious and less wholesome aspects.

HIGHLIGHTS IN THE HISTORY OF THE ACC:

1851 How dare they?

The schooner *America* crosses the Atlantic to Great Britain. Initially, the yacht's fearsome reputation deters competition until a journalist from *The Times* newspaper shames British yachtsmen into accepting the challenge, deriding them for allowing "the illustrious stranger to return with the proud boast to the New World that she had flung down the gauntlet to England, Ireland, and Scotland, and not one had been found to take it up." It works, and a race is arranged around the Isle of Wight organized by the Royal Yacht Squadron (RYS) offering a 'Cup of 100 Sovereigns' – now known as the '100 Guinea Cup' – to the victor. *America* competes in the race on behalf of the New York Yacht Club (NYYC) and defeats a fleet of fourteen prime British yachts to win the trophy. The victors return to New York offering the cup to the NYYC in 1857, as a 'Deed of Gift' with the intention that it should represent "a perpetual challenge cup for friendly competition between nations". The America's Cup is born.

1870 Have a nice day... and goodbye!

The first British challenger arrives in America, but James Ashbury on *Cambria*, representing the Royal Thames yacht Club (RTYC), has no success racing against fourteen American yachts, finishing 10th out of 15 on corrected time.

1871 Sulking over the silverware

Ashbury returns to challenge with a customized racing yacht, *Livonia*, built for the express purpose of winning the cup, but refuses to race more than one opponent. Lawyers become involved and the NYYC eventually concedes, but provides four candidates to race against *Livonia* while retaining the right to choose their defending yacht on each morning of racing. The American yachts *Columbia* and *Sappho* triumph and a bitter Ashbury returns to Britain. The multi-defence format is abandoned and Match Racing is introduced to the ACC.

1885 Thank you so much!

Sir Richard Sutton and Genesta challenge for the ACC and win the first race after the defender, *Puritan*, is disqualified from racing for a rule infringement. Sutton, however, forfeits this victory, claiming: "We have come here to race, not to parade victory on our own." American yachtsmen praise Sutton for this show of sportsmanship and then swiftly defeat *Genesta* in the following two races.

1895 Are we all playing the same game?

The Earl of Dunraven and *Valkyrie III* are beaten in the first race and immediately accuse the American opponent, *Defender*, of sailing outside the measurement rules of the ACC: an accusation that is dismissed. During the second race, *Valkyrie III* manoeuvres to avoid a spectator boat and rams *Defender*. Dunraven continues sailing and wins the race, but is disqualified for the earlier collision. On the third race, Dunraven sails to the start line but abandons the race and returns to Britain publicly accusing the defenders of cheating.

1899–1930 Long-suffering Lipton

During this period, Sir Thomas Lipton – a grocer, rubber and tea plantation owner, and self-made millionaire – launched five unsuccessful challenge

previous page *British tea-baron, Sir Thomas Lipton, made five challenges for the Cup between 1899 and 1930. The foredeck crew on his first America's Cup yacht,* Shamrock, *keep an eye on a fearless and agile photographer.*

above *In 1983, the unbeatable Aussie combination of businessman, Alan Bond with skipper, Jean Bertrand and yacht designer, Ben Lexcen, took the Cup from America for the first time in 132 years with 12 Metre,* Australia II.

next page *The gloves come off in the five-minute, pre-start period during Race 1 of the Louis Vuitton semi-finals in Auckland. Intimidation, forcing a penalty on your opponent and an advantageous position for the first leg are paramount.* One World (USA-67) *went on to beat* Prada.

Break her (*Shamrock IV*) up, Bob, and burn her in your fireplace! I never want to see this boat again

Sir Thomas Lipton to Bob Jacob (owner of a New York shipyard) after failing to win the America's Cup in 1920 on his fourth and penultimate attempt

attempts with a series of yachts called *Shamrock*. His nemesis in the ACC was the outstanding American helmsman, Charlie Barr. At 82 years old, Lipton made his final challenge for the cup on *Shamrock V* as the ACC moved its base from New York to Newport, Rhode Island and was outclassed by Harold Vanderbilt on the advanced J Class yacht, *Enterprise*.

1934 Protests and pay disputes
British aircraft designer and manufacturer Sir Tommy Sopwith challenges with the super-fast J Class yacht, *Endeavour*, and provides a serious threat for the defender, Vanderbilt, and his amateur crew on *Rainbow*. Sopwith wins the first two races, but a disallowed protest against *Rainbow* and a crew striking for a salary increase prevent him from achieving victory.

1937 *Ranger*, the unstoppable racing machine
Unnerved by the strength of Britain's challenge in 1934, Vanderbilt swore to defend the cup effectively. The result was a super-J Class beast of a boat: *Ranger*, a yacht designed after rigorous tank and wind tunnel testing, and built using the latest materials and technology. The ACC had entered a new era and Sopwith's second challenge with *Endeavour II* stood little chance of success. After the victorious defence, Vanderbilt questioned this leap in racing yacht design: "Was *Ranger* so good that she killed the class and scared off the others?"

1958 And after the break…
ACC racing recommences after a 21-year suspension. In the austere post-World War II period, J Class-sized budgets became unsustainable and the International 12 Metre Class was introduced, reducing ACC yachts from 65ft (19.81m) to 44ft (13.41m), effectively cutting down crew numbers and build costs.

1983 An Australian shake-up
The Louis Vuitton Cup (LVC) series is introduced as a method of selecting a challenger to face the defender in the ACC. *Australia II* proves to be unbeatable and wins the challenger series. The Australian team introduces the 'modesty skirt' hiding the yacht's radical winged keel behind a screen each time she is lifted from the water. Dennis Connor defends for America with *Liberty* and the seven races of ACC are tight with the score at 3-3 before the final race. During Race 7, *Australia II* overtakes *Liberty* on the final upwind leg and removes the Cup from America for the first time in 132 years.

1987 Connor to the rescue
Dennis Connor challenges on behalf of the San Diego Yacht Club with *Stars & Stripes*. The highly motivated team easily defeat *Kookaburra III* in Fremantle, Australia, and the cup returns to America. This edition of the ACC is the debut for New Zealand, challenging with *KiwiMagic*.

1988 Court cases + catamaran = Cup chaos

New Zealand banker, Michael Fay, exploits a loophole in the 'Deed of Gift' to launch a 'rogue challenge.' After a legal squabble over the legitimacy of the challenge, the Supreme Court in New York rules that the ACC should be raced and Fay arrives in America with a 90ft (27.43m) monohull, *New Zealand*. Connor and the San Diego Yacht Club respond with *Stars & Stripes*, a 55ft (16.76m) catamaran and the competitors return to court as the *New Zealand*ers insist that their opponent should race in a similar design of yacht. The court insists that the challenge should continue and Fay's team are beaten by the faster, American multihull.

1992 Finally, a formula

The standardized America's Cup Class of yacht is introduced. Bill Koch heads the defence with *America3* and successfully triumphs over the Italian challenge from *Il Moro de Venezia*, skippered by American Paul Cayard.

1995 The Blake and Coutts phenomenon

New Zealand win 42 races from 43 starts with *Black Magic* during the LVC. The Kiwi partnership of Sir Peter Blake and Russell Coutts defeat Dennis Connor and *Young America*. The ACC leaves San Diego for the Southern Hemisphere again.

2000 A Kiwi clean sweep

A decisive ACC victory for *Team New Zealand* with Blake and Coutts beating Italy's *Luna Rossa* 4–0: the Cup remains in Auckland. Confidence on board *Team New Zealand* is so high that Coutts hands the helm to his 26-year-old understudy, Dean Barker, for the final race.

2003 The tycoon frenzy

Russell Coutts and Brad Butterworth leave the New Zealand camp to join Ernesto Bertarelli and his new Swiss team, *Alinghi*. During the four months of racing in LVC, *Alinghi* scores 23 wins from 26 starts, defeating *Oracle BMW* of the American software mogul Larry Ellison. During the ACC, *Alinghi* faces the defender, *Team New Zealand* and the Kiwi team suffer severe gear failure, forcing them to retire from two races, leaving *Alinghi* to win the ACC with a clean sweep of 5-0. The cup heads back to Europe for the first time in 149 years.

2007 The 32nd ACC: The next 'Act'

The incumbent Swiss yacht club, Société Nautique de Genève (SNG), is challenged by the Golden Gate Yacht Club and the 32nd ACC begins. Bertarelli and his team choose the Spanish town of Valencia as the location and create a new three-year format of races. The Swiss team's former skipper, Russell Coutts, leaves *Alinghi* and is forbidden to compete in the cup for any of the teams. The ACC attracts eleven challengers with debut appearances from the Republic of South Africa and China.

It is a business and we, in England, who sail our yachts because we love sailing, can never win the America's Cup until we make it a business too

Sir Tommy Sopwith after defeat in two consecutive America's Cup Challenges

Things to do on an America's Cup yacht

Current ACC yachts race with a crew of seventeen: each team will divide the duties onboard according to the skills and strengths of the crew, but a 'typical' set-up for a yacht would be:

1/2. Tactician/Strategist

The intelligence-gathering core of the 'afterguard' (the generic term for the collection of expertise at the aft end of a boat). They will assess information from the Helmsman, Navigator and sail Trimmers, then combine this with their own observations of wind direction and the yacht's position relative to the competition and formulate a strategy for the race. The real talent is to successfully juggle immediate tactics and the effect these will have later in the race.

3. Navigator

Passes position information to the Helmsman, Strategist and Tactician.

4. Helmsman

Often the skipper of the boat, he has the overriding decision on tactics and must ensure the boat is sailing at its optimum speed and is manoeuvring effectively. On some ACC yachts, there may be two helmsmen: one for starting the race and a second for sailing the course. "A skipper's role is managing director on board," maintains Chris Dickson, skipper of *BMW Oracle* for the 2007 ACC. "I need accurate information in a timely fashion, presented in a clear way to enable the right decision to be made."

5. Traveller

Controls the mainsheet traveller dictating upwind speed.

6. Runners

Work the running backstays and controls the mast bend. In constant communication with Helmsman and Trimmers to maximize sail shape and the subsequent boat speed.

7. Mainsail Trimmer

Responsible for the position of the mainsail. Works with the Helmsman to maintain the maximum speed on every point of sail.

8. Mainsail Grinder

Controls the winch pedestal – or 'coffee grinder' – for the mainsail. Works directly to the commands of the Mainsail Trimmer.

opposite *Two crewmen on the current Cup defender,* Alinghi, *prepare to drop the jib while a third inspects the 'sewer': the most uncomfortable and stomach-churning place to find yourself on any racing yacht.*

below *Concentration for trimmer, Lorenzo Mazza, and tactician, Torben Grael (in black hat) on Italy's* Prada Challenge, *during the 2002 Louis Vuitton Cup quarter finals in the Hauraki Gulf, New Zealand. For the most efficient sheeting angles, a working jib sheet is loaded on to the winch 'wrong way round'.*

next page *Nerves of steel, an accurate watch and an advanced sense of balance for the bowman of French America's Cup contender,* K-Challenge, *as they take on the defender,* Alinghi, *at the start of Louis Vuitton Act 2 off Valencia in October 2004.*

Men in a ship are always looking up, and men onshore are usually looking down

John Masefield (1878-1987), poet and novelist

9/10. Headsail Trimmers

Directly control the upwind and downwind headsails and the critical 'height' (ability of sailing close to the wind) of the boat and overall speeds when sailing off the wind.

11/12. Grinders

Work the winch pedestals for the headsail sheets and all the halyards. They grind to the commands of the Headsail Trimmers during tacks and gybes and to the orders of the Mast and Pit for hoisting sails. Consistently in demand during a race, the job is physically demanding and Grinders are often the largest crewmembers on board. Usually they will be members of the informal Federation of Grinders (FOG) who, with the FDU (see below), represent the 'grunt' element of an ACC yacht.

13. Mast

His extra weight and strength on the halyards speeds sail hoists. During sail drops and gybing manoeuvres he will assist the foredeck crew.

14. Pit

Controls operations at the front of the boat co-ordinating sail changes and will assist the Grinders. He is also a link between the afterguard and the foredeck crew.

15. Sewer

As part of the foredeck crew, he will assist on deck during sail changes and manoeuvres, but his primary function is to re-pack and stow sails after a drop and prepare sails pre-hoist. Although he will receive help from the Mast, Pit and Mid-bow, he will spend extended periods alone below decks in cramped, damp and – when the boat is being driven hard – nauseous conditions.

16. Mid-bow

Acts as back-up to the Bowman and will assist Sewer, Pit and Mast when needed. Requires agility, stamina, a thick skin and an ability to follow orders without question.

17. Bowman

Possibly the busiest position on an ACC boat – brains and brawn combined. At the beginning of a race he must keep the Helmsman informed of the distance to the start line via hand signals and continue to advise the afterguard of any overlaps throughout the race. An error or misjudgement can fatally jeopardize a race. He is responsible for connecting sheets and halyards to the headsails during sail changes and is in sole charge of the outboard end of the spinnaker pole. He is usually the appointed spokesman of a yacht's Foredeck Union (FDU) with a membership comprising Mid-bow, Mast, Sewer and occasionally – but not always – Pit.

How to win

With a three-lap race course of slightly less than nineteen nautical miles, the 32nd ACC aims to provide close racing, regardless of differing crew quality between teams, and should prevent a competitor with a superior boat design from dominating on pure speed capabilities. The windward-leeward legs are of restricted length to reduce the chance of a faster design developing an unassailable lead and disappearing over the horizon, while the course covers enough distance to ensure that a yacht with an exceptionally skilled crew will not tyrannize an opponent on tactics alone. All very democratic… in theory.

An ACC race can be split into three sections: the Start, the Windward legs and the Leeward legs – totally distinct territories offering many different, tactical opportunities.

Start: Ten minutes before the start of a race as the yachts ready themselves near the starting area, a warning gun will be fired. This is a signal for crews to transfer any unwanted sails and equipment on to speedboats standing by. As the shore crew remove this excess weight from the yacht, the afterguard will be receiving final data from their dedicated weather analysts and last minute instructions from the team's coaches.

Five minutes before the start, a second gun is fired signalling the 'Pre-Start' period. The yachts are now forbidden any further outside assistance and a communication blackout is imposed. This period is an opportunity for a team to force their opponent into an error or a rule infringement and destroy their confidence while striving to gain the most favourable start. Although one of the greatest skills of a helmsman is the ability to steer his yacht across the start line milliseconds after the cannon fires, the primary objective is to seize an advantageous position for the

right *New Zealand feel the squeeze from* +39 Challenge *and* Luna Rossa Challenge *(Prada), two of Italy's three challengers for the 2007 America's Cup.*

When you start to beat the big boys, you have to be prepared and get a lawyer

Magnus Holmberg, skipper of Sweden's *Victory Challenge* on being disqualified after winning Louis Vuitton Act 5 in June 2005

Fly
TOYOTA
www.emirates.com
TOYOTA
NEW ZEALAND
Fly Emirates
NEW ZEALAND
Fly Emirates
PRADA
+39

upwind leg to the first windward mark. Gaining this objective provides the excitement immediately before the start as the yachts dance around each other, jousting for pole position. One of the final reports passed to the afterguard before the pre-start will have been an evaluation of any likely change in wind direction during the first leg. Crossing the start line first is not always an asset – determining the first wind shift is crucial.

Windward: The leading boat on an upwind leg will normally have the advantage. The team can bury the trailing yacht in their wind shadow and pin them down by mirroring each manoeuvre as the chasing yacht attempts to break free and find fresh breeze away from the turbulent, 'dirty air' in the wake of the lead boat.

The second and third windward legs, however, allow the trailing yacht to break clear of the leader. Instead of having both yachts round the same leeward mark, they pass through a gate of approximately six boat lengths in width at the leeward limit of the course; one yacht turns to port and the other to starboard. Splitting from the lead yacht and sailing upwind in clear air alters the entire complexion of the race.

Leeward: Sailing downwind, the trailing boat is able to disrupt the leader's advantage and – if the boats are close – control the race through use of their wind shadow and overlap. In the 32nd ACC, the final leg to the finish line is leeward and the final result can be overturned in the closing minutes of a race.

above *Things to avoid during a race… A spinnaker explodes and rips across the sail's width. The windseeker on the trailing yacht is holding on to his yacht's port jumper strut: these short, forward-angled spreaders provide support for the top of the mast, but can snag and tear spinnakers during a poorly executed gybe.*

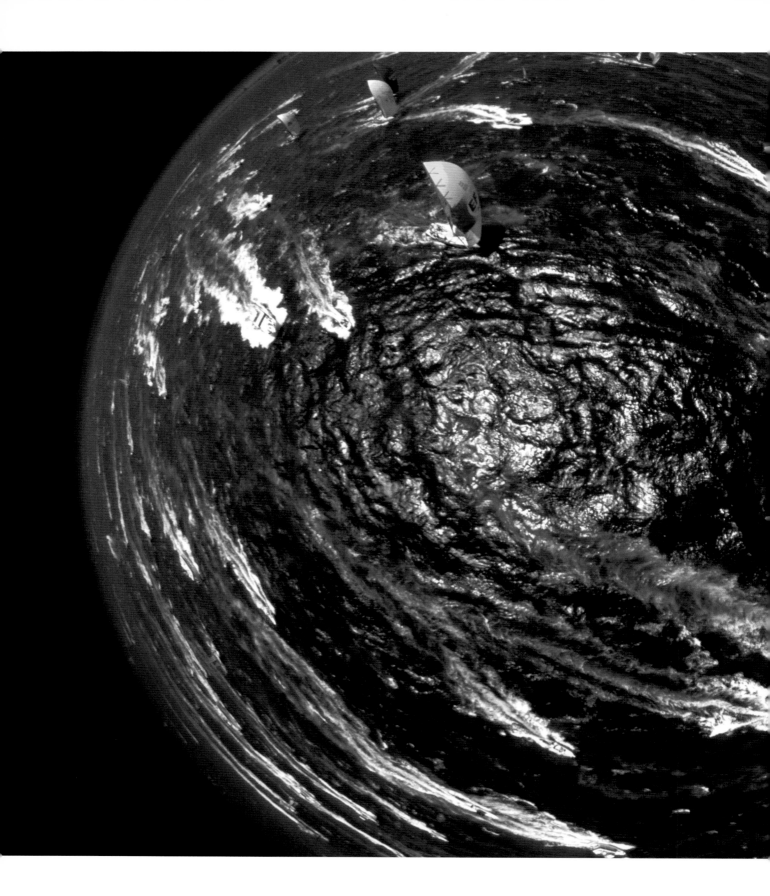

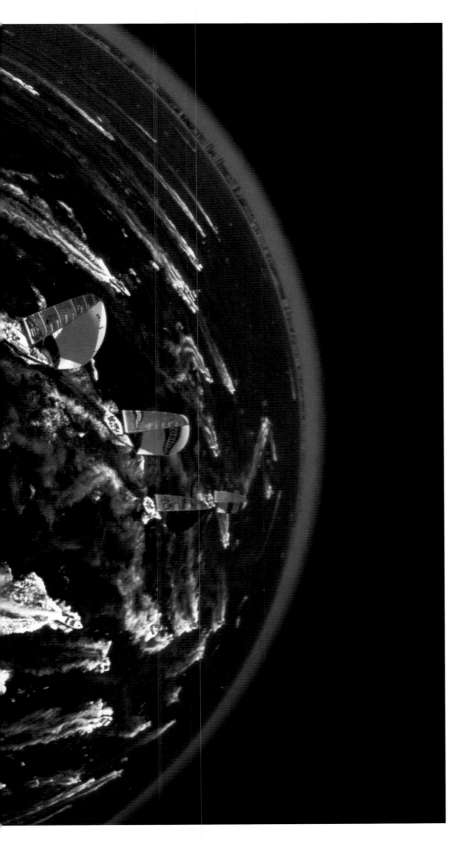

3

The Volvo Ocean Race

- THE BIG ONE

- OFFSHORE MADNESS?

- DEEP SEA STORIES

The big one

The Volvo Ocean Race – as the former Whitbread Race has been known since 2001 – captures public imagination more than any other round-the-world sailing event. This is due, in part, to well managed media surrounding the race and access to the competitors at nine stopover ports during the circumnavigation. An offshore race can often alienate spectators when the fleet of yachts are at sea for long periods in a remote environment that few yachtsmen have ever experienced. The intense tactics, the constant evaluation of weather systems and fanatical attention to sustaining high speeds can seem alien to the lay-sailor. However, the Volvo Ocean Race is, above all, about human endeavour and hardship; almost all sailors can connect in some way with the teams battling gales in distant oceans and for this reason, it is frequently the stories from the race, rather than the overall results, that enthral the land-based spectator.

Advances in technology have not softened the challenge facing teams in the 2005-06 Volvo Ocean Race. The ability to compress onboard video footage and stream these images ashore from the high latitudes of the Southern Ocean does not diminish a hostile and potentially lethal environment. Likewise, weather data fed to the race yachts and a 24-hour satellite tracking system logging the fleet's course around the globe are essential, but these features are little more than modern novelties when conditions deteriorate on a deep-ocean racing yacht.

Freeze-dried food, satellite connections with onshore medical staff, high-tech foul weather clothing and a carefully calculated calorie intake, boosted for the colder legs of the race, were unknown to competitors in the earlier editions of the event. Today's Volvo Ocean Race sailors may benefit from better communications and more enlightened ideas on personal safety and onboard conditions, but the pressure to race hard is more powerful than ever. Corporate sponsorship, professionalism and the media spotlight combine to push teams to their limit in yachts customized to break speed records.

44

right *Rothmans buries her bow during the 1989–90 Whitbread race. Skippered by Britain's Lawrie Smith, the yacht finished 4th in a fleet of 21 entrants and recorded a blistering average speed of 19.9 knots over a 90-minute period on Leg 2 between Uruguay, South America, and Fremantle, Australia.*

previous page *The fleet leaves Fort Lauderdale, Florida, during the 1997–98 Whitbread Race. A succession of protests, resignations and a disqualification dominated the seventh edition of the race.*

No man will be a sailor who has contrivance enough to get himself into jail; for being in a ship is being in jail, with the chance of being drowned [...]. A man in jail has more room, better food, and commonly better company.

Samuel Johnson (1709–1784), English writer, critic and landlubber

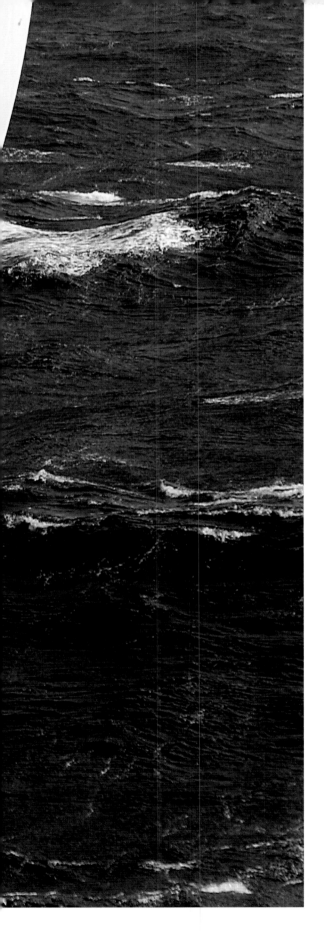

Offshore madness

During the 1960s, ocean racing became the chosen sport for sailors seeking fresh offshore challenges. In 1967, Sir Francis Chichester completed the first single-handed circumnavigation of the world, stopping only once in Australia, while two years later, Sir Robin Knox-Johnston became the first solo sailor to circle the planet non-stop in The Golden Globe Race. In France, meanwhile, Eric Tabarly was awarded the Legion of Honour by President Charles de Gaulle for his victory in the 1964 OSTAR single-handed race across the North Atlantic, but no event existed for yachtsmen craving fully crewed ocean racing.

The prospect of a round-the-world yacht race aroused intense scepticism. At this time, fewer than ten private yachts had rounded Cape Horn, while the Golden Globe Race of 1968 saw only one competitor finish from eight entrants and produced a catalogue of disasters, capsizes and a mid-Atlantic suicide. Who would underwrite and organize such folly?

The ocean-going environment of hardship, danger and endurance had a provocative appeal for at least one section of the seafaring community: the Royal Navy. In association with British brewing giant Whitbread, the Navy formulated a framework for the first fully crewed, competitive, circumnavigation. On 8 September 1973, seventeen yachts from seven nations with a total of 167 crew started the first Whitbread Round The World Race off Portsmouth, southern England.

The race has always provided drama and, sometimes, tragedy; the modern Volvo Ocean Race continues to attract world class sailors and a global following. From the earliest editions of the race it became clear that the Whitbread was an exceptional challenge and it continues to generate extraordinary stories of courage, determination and ingenuity. The race may also be one of the few sporting events where competitors have been arrested on suspicion of espionage and a yacht has been disqualified for carrying radioactive waste!

left *The bowman of* Amer Sports One *wrestles with the spinnaker's tack fitting as the yacht powers downwind during the 2001–02 Volvo Ocean Race. A total of three sailors were lost overboard during the first Whitbread race in 1973–74 and crew safety is a constant anxiety for competitors in deep-ocean events.*

next page *Volvo 60,* Assa Abloy, *surfs as her crew cling on during a power reach in the 2001–02 Volvo Ocean Race. The stress loads on the yacht's mast, rigging, sails and fittings must be constantly monitored to prevent breakages and maintain the delicate balance between speed and boat preservation.*

Deep sea stories

A summary of the human drama, turmoil and theatrics in the Whitbread and Volvo races from 1973 to 2002:

1973–74: A dangerous and deadly debut

Italian yacht *Tauranga* suffers sail damage in 50-knot winds during Leg 2 of the race between Cape Town, South Africa, and Sydney, Australia. Crewman Paul Waterhouse heads to the foredeck and is knocked unconscious as he is thrown to the deck: lying on the jib, a second gust picks up the sail and Waterhouse is flung overboard. The crew are unable to locate him.

Less than a week later, French ketch *33 Export* is caught in a gale. Massive waves sweep the 60ft yacht's decks and crewman Dominique Guilett is washed overboard when his harness snaps. Guilett becomes the second fatality of the race.

After leaving Sydney on Leg 3 bound for Rio de Janeiro, Brazil, Bernie Hosking is thrown overboard from *Great Britain II* during a storm that nearly dismasts the 77ft ketch. On Leg 1, Hosking was lost overboard en route to Cape Town and the crew recovered him, but the Pacific Ocean refused to give the yachtsman up.

Winner: *Sayula II* (Mexico)

1977–78: Luck, injuries and extreme bravery

On the second leg of the race, between Cape Town and Auckland, New Zealand, Bill Abram is flung over the side of *Heath's Condor* while not attached by a safety harness. The crew immediately lose sight of Abram behind tall waves, but a group of albatross are spotted circling in the distance. The object of their interest is a very fortunate Abram who is soon recovered by his crewmates.

On *Great Britain II*, Nick Dunlop is trapped when the spinnaker guy becomes wrapped around his waist. Before the line is cut, the force generated by the sail squeezes Dunlop until the blood vessels in his eyes rupture. Any attempts to move Dunlop produce screams of agony, but he sustains no permanent injuries.

In the Roaring Forties on Leg 3 between Auckland and Rio, *33 Export* broaches and Eric Letrosne fractures a leg when he is slammed into the guardrails. The crew radio Dr Jean Louis Sarbarly on the nearby yacht, *Japy-Hermes*, and after a diagnosis over the VHF, Sarbarly braves freezing Southern Ocean water, swims across to *33 Export* and treats Letrosne.

French yacht *Pen Duick VI* is disqualified from the race when it is found that her heavy keel is weighted with depleted uranium (twice as heavy as lead).

Winner: *Flyer* (Netherlands)

below: *Shortly before the finish of Leg 2 of the 1985–86 Whitbread,* Lion New Zealand *collided with a whale. With serious damage to the rudder, skipper, Peter Blake nursed the yacht to the Auckland finish line arriving in 4th place.*

The sea is dangerous and its storms terrible – but these obstacles have never been sufficient reason to remain ashore.

Ferdinand Magellan (c.1480–1521), Portuguese explorer and circumnavigator

1981–82: Dismastings and double agents

As the yachts head down through the Atlantic on Leg 1, New Zealand entry *Ceramco NZ* dismasts 150 miles north of Ascension Island. They continue racing with a jury rig and arrive in Cape Town in 18th place (out of 26).

South African crew racing on the Italian yacht *Vivanapoli* are arrested on suspicion of espionage when the boat is boarded by personnel from an Angolan gunboat. The Italian embassy eventually secures their release from prison.

On Leg 2 between Cape Town and Auckland, *33 Export* dismasts and diverts to the remote and barren Kerguelen Islands in the high latitudes of the Indian Ocean to make repairs.

Spanish entry *Licor* dismasts on Leg 3 in a 60-knot Pacific Ocean gale. The crew continue under jury rig and sail round Cape Horn to the next stopover in Mar del Plata, Argentina. *Gauloises II* also dismasts on Leg 3, but the yacht retires to Tahiti.

With a comfortable lead on the final leg of the race, *Flyer* runs aground on the notorious Shingles Bank within a few miles of the finish. The crew succeed in freeing the yacht on an ebb tide and sail the final twelve miles to Portsmouth.

Winner: *Flyer* (Netherlands)

below *Swedish entry,* The Card, *suffered a broach in the Indian Ocean's high latitudes during Leg 2 of the 1989–90 race. Skipper Dr. Roger Nilson used the onboard tool kit to make a cast for the broken arm of a French crewmember injured when the yacht was knocked flat.*

52

above *Whitbread 60,* Tokio, *was dismasted off the coast of Brazil during the 1993–94 Whitbread Race and headed into the port of Santos. Chris Dickson and his crew repaired the mast within thirty-six hours before setting back out to sea and sailing to rejoin the fleet in Fort Lauderdale, Florida.*

1985–86: Scuba diving and mast climbing in the Southern Ocean

Atlantic Privateer dismasts 500 miles from Cape Town on Leg 1 and her jury rig fails soon afterwards forcing the crew to sail the boat under engine power. *Drum* suffers drastic delamination in vicious gales shortly after crossing the Equator and a hull inspection in South Africa reveals that the keel is in danger of falling off the bottom of the boat.

Three days into Leg 3 between Auckland and Punta del Este, Uruguay, *NZI Enterprise* breaks her mast in two places and retires to the Chatham Islands.

A spinnaker sail bag is swept off the deck of *Drum* and becomes tangled around the propeller. Crewman Magnus Olsson, climbs into scuba gear and dives over the side attached to a tether, but is knocked unconscious by the stern of the pitching boat and the crew haul him back onboard. Olsson is uninjured and the bag is eventually removed by dragging a line along the yacht's hull until the obstruction is snagged.

Ed Danby is sent to the top of the mast on *Lion New Zealand* to retrieve a spinnaker that is flying from its halyard only. The attachment of the bosun's chair fails and Danby is left clinging to the top spreaders until a second crewman is hauled aloft and brings him down to deck level.

Winner: *L'Esprit d'Equipe* **(France)**

1989–90: Tragedy onshore and offshore

The first all-women crew enter the race with *Maiden*, skippered by Britain's Tracy Edwards.

Two deaths occur onshore during the stopover at the end of Leg 1 from Southampton to Punta del Este, Uruguay: Alexei Grishschenko, co-skipper of the Russian entry, *Fazisi*, commits suicide and Janne Gustaffson, a crewmember of *The Card*, is killed in a motorcycle accident.

On the second leg from Uruguay to Fremantle, Australia, a crewman on *Fortuna Extra Lights* is washed overboard. Although he is not wearing a safety harness, his radio locator enables the crew to recover him.

In the Indian Ocean, *Creightons Naturally* loses two crewmen overboard in two consecutive crash gybes. Bart van den Dwey is located after forty-five minutes in freezing water and Tony Phillips is found after a further quarter of an hour. Three hours of CPR fail to resuscitate Phillips.

After rounding Cape Horn, the keel falls off Finnish yacht, *Martela OF*, as she sails north along the coast of South America. The crew manage to send a 'Mayday' before the yacht inverts totally and the radio equipment fails. *Merit* and *Charles Jourdan* divert to the stricken yacht's position and rescue the crew from an upturned hull.

Winner: *Steinlager 2*

1993–94: Tough crews and tender boats

Two classes race; the larger Maxi class and the Whitbread 60 (W60).

Heading west across the Atlantic from Southampton to Punta del Este, Spanish yacht *Fortuna* dismasts early in Leg 1 and the team retire from the race. The yacht's skipper, Lawrie Smith, takes over the top spot on *Intrum Justicia* at the Uruguayan stopover.

On the longest, second leg from South America to Fremantle, *NZ Endeavour*, skippered by Grant Dalton, broaches and snaps her mizzen mast. Italian W60, *Brooksfield*, breaks her rudder shaft and 3 tons of water pour through the gaping hole below the waterline. The crew send an SOS and Dennis Connor's *Winston* and Smith's *Intrum Justicia* immediately divert to the sinking yacht's position. Twelve hours after the distress signal, the first yacht to reach *Brooksfield* is French entrant, *La Poste*, skippered by Eric Tabarly. *La Poste* remains on standby in 60-knot winds until two US Navy ships rendezvous mid-ocean and escort the mortally wounded yacht to port.

The attrition of the race begins to show on Leg 5 between Uruguay and Fort Lauderdale, Florida, as many of the W60 fleet suffer severe delamination, causing a dangerous weakening of the hull. British entrant *Dolphin & Youth* diverts to Rio, fearing that the boat will disintegrate, while *NZ Endeavour* and *La Poste* make temporary repairs and continue to the US. Chris Dickson's W60, *Tokio*, is spared delamination, but dismasts and is forced to head for the Brazilian port of Santos. In thirty-six hours, Dickson's crew repair the broken mast and head for America.

Winners: Maxi class: *New Zealand Endeavour*
W60 class: *Yamaha* (Japan/New Zealand)

above *No frills down below for the female crew of* EF Language *in the 2001–02 Volvo Ocean Race. In the limited space aboard a VO60, crew must 'hot-bunk': a crewmember coming off watch will crawl into the recently vacated bunk of a crewmember heading on deck for their turn on watch.*

above *Learning not to flinch when tons of ice-cold water pour aft along the decks is an essential asset to an offshore helmsman.*

1997–98: Big names and big trouble

The last edition of the race to bear the Whitbread title and the longest with nine legs in total, including short, sprint passages.

There is an early setback for Norwegian *Innovation Kvaerner*, when her generator explodes within sight of the Southampton start line.

Rudder damage on *BrunelSunergy* after striking a whale in the Atlantic forces the team to head for Recife, Brazil, to make repairs. Generally light winds and slow speeds on the 7,350-mile first leg to Cape Town cause food shortages on a number of boats. However, Lawrie Smith and British entry *Silk Cut* produce a record breaking 24-hour run of 417.2 miles. The yacht betters this record on Leg 2 sailing 449.1 miles at an average speed of 18.7 knots.

American skipper Paul Cayard wins Leg 1 on *EF Language*, silencing critics who believed that his success and experience in the America's Cup would be worthless in an offshore race.

Two boats cause controversy in the South African stopover; Chris Dickson resigns as skipper of *Toshiba*, commenting: "I would be letting myself down by continuing the campaign." Rumours of friction between

Dickson and the team's project manager, Dennis Connor, circulate. Also, the un-sponsored US entry of Dr Neil Bath pulls out due to lack of funding.

At the end of Leg 2 in Fremantle, Australia, two further team changes take place: the skipper of Dutch entry, *BrunelSunergy*, steps down after finishing last in the first two legs and is replaced by Olympic medallist Roy Heiner. Soon afterwards, co-skipper of *Chessie Racing*, Mark Fischer, resigns. When asked to comment on the tense atmosphere aboard the yacht, Fischer explained curtly: "On any boat during the heat of competition you get some normal friction between skipper and crew."

On the first 2,250-mile 'sprint' of the race, Leg 3 between Fremantle and Sydney, *Innovation Kvaerner* discovers potentially disastrous damage to the yacht's mast. Skipper Knut Frostad radios his shore team and a helicopter drops a repair kit to the yacht.

During the second 'sprint' leg between Sydney and Auckland, Dennis Connor joins the crew on *Toshiba* racing against his America's Cup rival, Paul Cayard, on *EF Language*. Connor protests against Cayard for failing to switch on his navigation lights after dark, claiming that this gave *EF Language* a tactical advantage in concealing her position. A protest jury is flown to New Zealand and Connor's claim is judged to be invalid.

Leaving the protests and intrigue in Auckland, the yachts head into the Southern Ocean for Leg 5 to São Sebastião, Brazil. Both *Silk Cut* and *EF Education* (sister ship to Cayard's *EF Language*) suffer mast and rigging failure 2,000 miles from the nearest land and are forced to limp cautiously to the Argentine port of Ushuaia, north-east of Cape Horn.

In Brazil, it is discovered that *Toshiba* started her engine and engaged reverse gear to free the yacht from a bed of kelp wrapped around the keel. Before crossing the finish line, the crew replaced a security seal specifically fitted by race officers in Auckland to reveal any evidence of the yacht's propeller shaft turning. As the team failed to inform the race committee of this action and even omitted to record the incident in the boat's log, *Toshiba* is disqualified from Leg 5.

Further protests marred Leg 7 between Fort Lauderdale and Baltimore when *EF Education* protest against *Toshiba* for failing to execute a 720° penalty turn after a port/starboard incident. The race jury uphold the protest and Connor's navigator, Andrew Cape, resigns describing the Whitbread as "a hard race and I have not especially enjoyed it."

A series of protests threatened to disrupt the final leg from La Rochelle, France, to Southampton, but – possibly weary of squabbling after a long and controversial race – all claims and procedures are dropped.

Winner: *EF Language* (Sweden)

2001–02: Less arguing and more racing

Re-named the Volvo Ocean Race, the event signifies a leap in offshore competitive sailing. Fierce rivalry is reflected in close racing and the outbreak of egos and internal politics witnessed in the previous race are avoided. Ocean racing enters a newer, faster and intensely combative era.

Winner: *Illbruck* (Germany)

left *Volvo 60 Illbruck – winner of the 2001–02 Volvo Ocean Race – glides past the lighthouse in Gothenburg, Sweden.*

4

Offshore Fully Crewed

The Fastnet Race

The biennial Fastnet Race is far from being the longest offshore racing event: the Cape Town to Rio Race traverses the South Atlantic covering 4,000 miles and the gruelling Trans-Pacific Yacht Race from Los Angeles to Honolulu, Hawaii, lasts between seven and eight days – over twice the usual length of the Fastnet. Nonetheless, the event has always been considered a *grand cru* offshore yacht race.

The Notice of Race for the 608-mile (978km) course is simple: "Cowes – Fastnet Rock – Plymouth", taking the racing fleet south-west from the start line off Cowes. After the yachts compress and bunch between Hurst Point and The Needles marking the end of the confined, opening stage of the race in The Solent between the Isle of Wight and mainland Britain, they head into the English Channel. The passage along Britain's southern coast takes the race past the headlands of Anvil Point, Portland Bill, Start Point and The Lizard before leaving Land's End to starboard and heading into the Celtic Sea. Yachts then head north-west for 180 nautical miles of open water to the lighthouse clinging on to Fastnet Rock off the southern tip of Ireland. Once round the rock, yachts head back across their outward route, rounding Bishop Rock Lighthouse to the south of the Isles of Scilly – 30 miles off Land's End – and on to the final leg and the finish line in Plymouth.

The history of the Fastnet contributes to its legendary status. Originated in 1925, the race appealed to amateur British yachtsmen and the early races were remarkable for the high level of retirements from the course: evidence of inexperienced crews, ancient and poorly equipped yachts and a tough route. During the 1930s, American and French yachts joined the racing fleet and quickly upstaged the British entrants, bringing a new spirit of competition to the event. Although the race is held in August – a period of high pressure and traditionally light winds – a gale during the 1931 Fastnet battered the fleet and one crewmember was lost overboard: a catastrophic episode, but a feature that firmly established the race as a rite of passage for offshore sailors.

The Fastnet Race won a senior place in sailing folklore during the disastrous 1979 edition of the event. During a brutal storm, the fleet of 303 yachts was smashed by hurricane-strength winds and monstrous seas. In total, twenty-four yachts were abandoned of which five sank and although fifteen sailors lost their lives, the extraordinary skill of rescue services resulted in 136 men and women being plucked from yachts and liferafts. The tragedy of the race and sheer terror and might of this storm is conveyed by the account of 17-year-old yachtsman, Matt Sheahan, sailing on his father's yacht, *Grimalkin*. Sheahan survived the gale in a liferaft although his father David was lost overboard – his body carried downwind away from the stricken yacht.

previous page *Slamming to windward across the Bass Strait, 47ft (14.3m)* Ausmaid *heads south to Tasmania in the 1997 Sydney–Hobart Race. Conscious of the wild conditions yachts can encounter offshore in the Bass Strait, entry documents for the race must include a "colour photograph of the boat under sail no older than twelve months and suitable for search and rescue purposes".*

opposite *Fastnet Rock off the southern tip of Ireland. For nineteenth-century Irish immigrants sailing to America, the rock was the final glimpse of home and became known as 'Ireland's Teardrop.' The lighthouse is now the mid-point turning mark of the biennial Fastnet Race – a rite of passage for offshore sailors.*

We heard the radio messages from the aeroplanes saying: "I've done my square search. I haven't found you, but DON'T WORRY – we'll be back and WE WILL FIND YOU!"

Robin Aisher, skipper of *Yeoman XXI*, in a BBC interview after his crew and yacht survived the tragic 1979 Fastnet Race

"Sometimes events are so big and get so out of control as to make you feel minuscule. Something deep within you realizes that there's absolutely nothing you can do about it. You almost go beyond a state of fear. The whole thing was completely and utterly overwhelming."

A tangible legacy of the 1979 race exists in the stringent qualifications and safety requirements demanded by the race organizers, the Royal Ocean Racing Club (RORC). To enter the Fastnet Race, a yacht's skipper and half of her crew must have already completed a 300-mile offshore race or a non-stop, offshore cruising passage of the same length. In addition, a first aid certificate is mandatory for two crewmembers on each yacht and half the crew must have received training in the use of liferafts. Ominously, all competitors must submit their 'Next of Kin' details before starting the race.

opposite *The death toll during gales in the tragic 1979 Fastnet Race reached fifteen. Trailing warps and sea anchors, the eighth and final crewmember waits to be hoisted from a badly stricken yacht.*

below *The challenge of the Fastnet Race attracts a broad range of entrants. Three different nationalities squeeze past the Needles, thirteen miles west of the start line during the early stages of the 2005 race.*

The Sydney–
Hobart Race

The 628-mile route of the annual Sydney–Hobart Race could easily appear in a luxury cruise brochure. Yachts leave Sydney Harbour on 26 December at the height of the Southern Hemisphere summer and sail across the 150 miles of the Bass Strait separating mainland Australia from the island of Tasmania. The race continues south past the stunning scenery of Tasmania's east coast until reaching Tasman Island and turning west into Storm Bay with a further 40 miles to the final destination at the city of Hobart. After rounding an old whaling station called Iron Pot, 11 miles of sailing along the Derwent River brings you to Battery Point in the island's capital city. However, this is the only feature that the brutal race shares with spending the Christmas holidays on a liner.

The Sydney–Hobart Race and its older, northern equivalent, the Fastnet Race, have a similar appeal for sailors. The event is open to a wide range of boats and attracts a broad spectrum of yachtsmen from serial ocean racers to offshore novices. The thrill of a passage through open ocean is topped by close racing along the coast of Tasmania and a vibrant welcome at the destination port. A perfect combination, perhaps, were it not for the narrow, shallow obstacle of the Bass Strait: an infamous and savage sea area littered with shipwrecks from the nineteenth century. The strait continues to wreak havoc with modern racing yachts as they sprint across this turbulent link separating the vast Indian Ocean from the plunging depths of the Tasman Basin. The Sydney–Hobart has a chilling history of destructive storms, damaged yachts and human fatalities. A gale during the 1984 edition of the race caused one death and compelled 104 of the 150 entrants to retire. Four years later, 119 yachts crossed the start line in Sydney Harbour and thirty-eight opted to retire before reaching Hobart. In 1993 a four-day gale sank two yachts and forced sixty-four entrants to retire.

While Northern Hemisphere yachtsmen regard the 1979 Fastnet Race as an offshore bogey-man, towering waves six storeys high and winds reaching 70mph during the 1998 Sydney–Hobart Race caused a catastrophic loss of life. In horrific conditions, seven boats were abandoned of which five sank, including the 52ft (15.8m) *Winston Churchill*, a veteran of the first Sydney–Hobart Race in 1945. Chris Winning, the yacht's skipper, described the horror after being recovered:

"The worst thing of the whole affair was that after we got into the liferaft and became separated from the others, the damned thing capsized twice on these great seas at night which is bloody frightening, let me tell you."

The sea is feline. It licks your feet –
its huge flanks purr very pleasant
for you; but it will crack your bones
and eat you, for all that, and wipe
the crimsoned foam from its jaws
as if nothing had happened.

Oliver Wendell Holmes (1809-1894), American physician and writer

previous page *After crossing the 150-mile wide Bass Strait, Sydney–Hobart yachts slide down the east coast of Tasmania and under 'the organ pipes' at Cape Raoul.*

above *Size is important, but it cannot guarantee a comfortable ride – the crew on 80ft (24.4m) maxi* Nicorette *braves the weather rail on the 2002 Sydney–Hobart. A big swell and high winds in the Bass Strait produced waterspouts and a severe pounding for the race fleet.*

opposite *The Sydney–Hobart 2004 claims a victim –* Yendys *hurtles past the liferaft of capsized and abandoned maxi yacht,* Skandia Wild Thing *off the coast of Tasmania.*

Twenty-four fixed-wing aircraft and six helicopters armed with heat-seeking equipment joined in a desperate hunt for sailors in a search area extending over 4,000 square nautical miles, successfully rescuing fifty-five yachtsmen. It is purely due to the speed, skill and bravery of the rescue services that the tragic death toll was limited to six.

The 1998 Sydney–Hobart Race illustrates that advances in technology, communications and – most importantly – weather forecasting cannot guarantee safety at sea or provide a protective scientific buffer of knowledge against the elements. Winner of the first race in 1945, the 34ft (10.3m) yacht *Rani* took a little over eleven days to complete the course with the skipper and crew spending much of the race stuffing bedding and blankets into gaping holes in the hull as the yacht's pine planks worked loose. Fifty-four years later, a water-ballasted, purpose-built racing machine, *Nokia*, sped from Sydney to Hobart in one day and twenty hours. The speed and durability of racing yachts has increased over time, but sailors still face an element that continues to show little respect for technological sophistication.

The Global Challenge: a ticket to ride

In 1971, Sir Chay Blyth became the first man to sail around the world non-stop west-about – against the prevailing winds and currents. Sailing downwind around the globe has always been the preferred route and Blyth's decision to beat upwind through hostile oceans into the endless waves rolling around the planet was not a popular choice. However, since his pioneering circumnavigation, Blyth has persuaded over 650 people to follow the perilous and uncomfortable 'wrong direction' route and pay a considerable amount of money for this honour.

The Global Challenge provides a 29,000-mile circumnavigation race for twelve, identical, 72ft (21.9m) yachts crewed by amateur yachtsmen with a professional skipper on board each boat. After crossing the start line off Portsmouth, England, the fleet spends just under nine months ploughing to windward with stopover ports in Argentina, New Zealand, Australia, South Africa, USA and France before returning to the UK and crossing the final finish line. There are few similarities between the Global Challenge and the Volvo Ocean Race, although both events involve a fully crewed circumnavigation and promote themselves as "the toughest yacht race in the world". Boats in the Volvo Ocean Race are stripped-down, super-light racing machines crewed by professionals with the sole purpose of circling the globe in 'the right direction' as fast as possible. Global Challenge yachts are wide and solid with the strength and capability to carry an amateur crew around the world 'the wrong way'.

The cost of joining the Global Challenge is another fundamental difference: £28,750 (approx. US$51,800 or 42,150Euros) will secure a place for the entire circumnavigation in the 2008–09 edition of the race and the event attracts crew from a diverse, international spectrum. Housewives, lawyers, students, company directors and plumbers have raced around the world with no prior sailing experience other than a pre-race training programme provided by Blyth's organisation. While the price of a place on board a Global Challenge yacht includes plenty of headroom and space with the use of a hot water shower in the freezing Southern Ocean, it also incorporates sailing through notoriously treacherous oceans with a collection of strangers. Mid-Atlantic gales, numbing cold, constant discomfort and exhaustion are tough to handle when sailing with an experienced, professional crew, but encountering extreme offshore conditions on board a yacht crewed by novices with predominantly land-based backgrounds is even more demanding.

Without doubt, lifelong bonds of friendship are forged through shared hardship during the Global Challenge. During the 2004–05 race, two crew on competing yachts became engaged over the VHF radio. This proposal is highly romantic and possibly unique, although the rules demand that the radio is left 'open' throughout the race and this deeply personal moment was eavesdropped upon by all 216 sailors in the twelve-boat fleet.

opposite *Constant discomfort, freezing conditions and a permanent adrenaline rush face Global Challenge crews during their 29,000-mile, nine-month, pay-as-you-go circumnavigation.*

next page *A Global Challenge crew succeeds in hoisting their fluorescent storm jib as the yacht pounds through the turbulent wind funnel of Cook Strait between North Island and South Island, New Zealand.*

He that would go to sea for pleasure, would go to hell for a pastime.

A sailing proverb

How many crew?
The Transat Jacques Vabre

The double-handed Transat Jacques Vabre race fills a gap in the Open class competitive calendar. Held every two years, the race is restricted to 60ft (18.28m) and 50ft (15.24m) Open class monohulls and multihulls. Normally, these yachts compete in fully crewed inshore races or race single-handed in transatlantic events. However, put two sailors on an IMOCA (International Monohull Open Class Association) or ORMA (Open Racing Multihull Association) 50- or 60-footer, and a new type of sailing evolves.

Open class solo sailors are an independent breed: pairing two of these solitary ocean wanderers on the same boat and challenging them to race from France to Brazil presents a unique set of circumstances. French trimaran ace Loïck Peyron explains:

"The difficulty [in a double-handed transatlantic race] is that you tend to push the boat to her limits as if there were a full crew on board, when in reality there are just two soloists."

This situation produces a thrilling spectacle for the spectator — greedily absorbing tales from the race track via television or the Internet — as the yachts hurtle into the Atlantic at full pace on the edge of control. In addition, the race starts in November, obliging the fleet to head immediately into strong winds from deep, low pressure systems charging towards Europe, before the yachts hook on to the trade winds and head for the equator. All the components for an epic contest are fused in the Transat Jacques Vabre.

above *The two crewmembers racing a 60ft trimaran are constantly active and alert for the two weeks at sea during the Transat Jacques Vabre race. Heavy commercial traffic in the English Channel and November gales in the Bay of Biscay can mean no sleep or hot food for the initial four days of racing as the yachts fly south towards the Equator. Jean-Luc Nelias and Loïck Peyron sailed* Belgacom *across the finish line taking 2nd place in 2003, completing the transatlantic race in less than twelve days.*

opposite top *Capable of beam reaching at 30 knots in 20-knot wind speeds, hand steering is essential. While autopilots can function effectively in flat water, a rapid human response is needed to control the boat, follow the 'wave train' and maximize speed in rough conditions.*

opposite bottom *Arguably the most extreme offshore sailing machines on the planet, ORMA 60 trimarans wait in the French port of Le Havre for the start of the 5,000-mile Transat Jacques Vabre race from France to Brazil. Meticulous pre-race preparation is vital to ensure the boats can be pushed hard through the North and South Atlantic.*

A race anatomy

Straight into the action: The race leaves Le Havre on the north coast of France over two days: the monohulls and 50ft trimarans are sent off first with the faster 60ft multihulls starting a day later. Heading west along the English Channel, the first hurdle will be the bulk of commercial traffic streaming down the coast. This hazard increases during the first night at sea as the fleet approach Ushant, the western extremity of France and a busy junction for shipping heading north and south along the continental coast.

Turning the corner into an early ambush: Once past Ushant, the Bay of Biscay can form a dangerous trap for the yachts. Cutting a fine line south across Biscay to clip Cape Finisterre – the western tip of Spain – competitors risk being forced deep into the bay by westerly winds and swells rolling in from the Atlantic. Misjudging the track across the bay can force yachts to tack north-west and escape into open waters as the more prudent boats slip past Finisterre and head towards the Azores archipelago; for some boats and crews the initial four days can be the most demanding part of the race. Rough weather and vital early tactical decisions place immense pressure on man and machine, preventing crews from developing any offshore racing rhythm of sleeping and eating.

Trade Winds and tactics: The boats will soon increase speed as they link with the North Atlantic trade winds off the coast of Portugal, sailing downwind, pushed south by the north-west breeze. The two Atlantic archipelagos of the Canary Islands and the Cape Verde Islands off the coast of Africa are crucial stages of the race: threading through the islands or sailing to leeward can leave a boat stalled in windless conditions. Heading close inshore may also increase the risk of a night-collision with small local fishing boats, many of which carry no navigation lights.

Down in the Doldrums: Before crossing the equator and heading into the Southern Hemisphere, the racing fleet must traverse the Doldrums – an area where good judgement can produce massive gains. The Doldrums area is a constantly shifting band of light and fickle winds interspersed with savage squalls. Racing crews will have been studying satellite weather information for this area since shortly after crossing the start line, as finding the narrowest section of the Doldrums and ensuring a swift transition southward, is supremely important. Evaluating meteorological data for the area is notoriously difficult and poor judgement or inaccurate weather forecasting can leave a yacht drifting slowly south with slack sails.

Drag racing to the finish: Once through the Doldrums barrier, the monohulls will head west towards Brazil, hooking into the south-east trade winds. Downwind speed and pushing the boat hard become the

above *The intense competition and rivalry of the Transat Jacques Vabre race pushes both man and machine to the limit. Inaccurate weather data, a minor tactical error forced by fatigue, gear failure or plain bad luck can result in disappointment and – occasionally – disaster.*

determining factor of the race. At this stage, thorough pre-race preparation of the boat becomes critical to enable the crew to drive the boat hard with the maximum sail area. Any equipment failure during this high-speed drag race towards the Brazilian coast can prove catastrophic and vital time will be lost as the crew is forced to slow down and make repairs. A 60ft monohull will complete the 4,500-mile race in approximately sixteen days and is likely to average speeds of 11 knots.

After exiting the Doldrums, the 60ft multihulls are sent further south to round the remote mid-Atlantic turning mark of Ascension Island before heading west to the finish line off Salvador de Bahia. Capable of average speeds hovering around 15 knots, the ORMA multihulls will still complete the extended 5,000-mile race course one or two days ahead of the leading monohull.

5

Solo Sailing Pioneers

- THE PIONEERS

- THE GOLDEN GLOBE

The pioneers

Joshua Slocum (1844–1909) consistently rejected any idea that his round-the-world, single-handed voyage on *Spray* was an historic, pioneering journey. The proud and professional commercial sailor regarded the three-year circumnavigation between 1895 and 1898 as an exercise in seamanship and offshore tourism: "If the *Spray* discovered no continents on her voyage, it may be that there are no more continents to be discovered. To find one's way to lands already discovered is a good thing and *Spray* made the discovery that even the worst sea is not so terrible to a well-appointed ship." The Canadian yachtsman's summary ignores extraordinary drama encountered during a voyage that included outrunning pirates off Gibraltar and successfully repelling two canoes filled with barefooted Indians in the Straits of Magellan by covering the 36ft sloop's decks with carpet-tacks.

Thirty years later, French sailor Alain Gerbault (1893–1942), a World War I fighter pilot, socialite and tennis maestro, arrived in Le Havre on the northern coast of France having completed a five-year, solo circumnavigation in *Firecrest*. The length of Gerbault's voyage reflects a strong relationship with the ocean, the independence that a yacht provides and the access this allows to remote, 'uncivilized' areas of the planet. While absorbing the beauty and culture of the Pacific Islands, Gerbault spent time mixing with exiled fellow countrymen and mysterious misfits scattered throughout French Polynesia. He also delayed departure if the chance of playing any sport arose; Gerbault defeated all his tennis opponents in Bermuda, Ascension Island and Durban, South Africa, while joining rugby games in Samoa and football matches in both the Cape Verde Archipelago and on Réunion, east of

I realized that I could not hope to arrive in time for the tennis tournament at Wimbledon.

Alain Gerbault's only regret after his five-year, solo circumnavigation (from *In Quest of The Sun*)

below *Chichester's 1966–67 circumnavigation followed the route used by clipper ships, sailing with the prevailing winds and currents from west to east around the world. Before his voyage on* Gypsy Moth IV, *only nine small yachts had circumnavigated the world via Cape Horn taking three years on average: Chichester's one-stop marathon took nine months.*

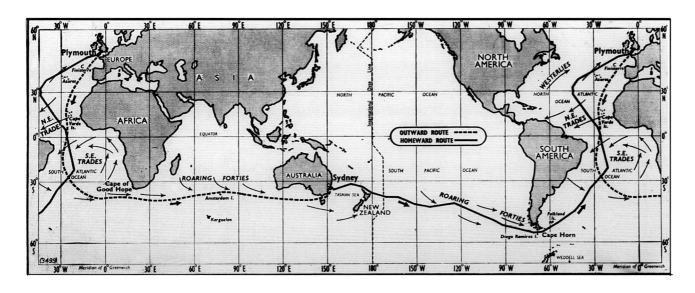

above *In 1924, French sailor, Alain Gerbault, sailed 39ft* Firecrest *into Le Havre after a five-year, single-handed circumnavigation. The flamboyant Frenchman constantly delayed his return to Europe and dreaded the lack of freedom and celebrity status waiting in France..*

previous page *"A real old ice-breaking boat. If she hit England, I'd be concerned for England..." was a Falmouth port official's description of Robin Knox-Johnston's 32ft ketch,* Suhaili, *shortly before the start of the Golden Globe single-handed non-stop round-the-world, race.*

Madagascar. The fearless French sailor also risked serious injury on Wallis Island in the Pacific during a contest that resembled a confusing hybrid of cricket and baseball.

Gerbault continued to delay his return to France by sheltering from North Atlantic storms and wintering in the Cape Verde Islands off Africa. He later recorded the dread and dislike for this eventual return to Europe: "But how readily would I have braved all dangers and difficulties, pumping [the bilges] day and night light-heartedly, if my objective had been new tropical isles and not France, where I expect an enthusiastic reception and a fame that was bound to curtail my liberty."

This colourful and buccaneering approach to solo sailing matured into a challenging sport in the 1960s with the heroic seamanship and navigational skills of Sir Francis Chichester (1901–1972). A confirmed adventurer, Chichester had already flown solo from Britain to Australia, continuing across the Tasman Sea and, finally, flying alone from Australia to Japan before switching from biplanes to boats. In 1960 he won the OSTAR (Observer Single-handed Transatlantic Race)

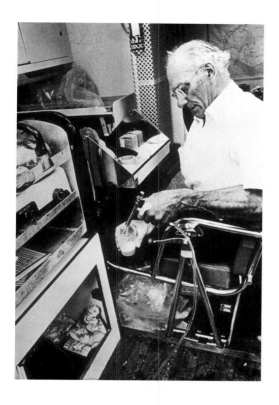

sailing *Gypsy Moth III* from Plymouth, England, to Newport, Rhode Island, and between 1966 and 1967 he completed a solo circumnavigation of the globe – including one stop over in Australia – on *Gypsy Moth IV*.

The entire concept for Chichester's circumnavigation had been audacious. When *Gypsy Moth IV* set off on her voyage, fewer than ten yachts had circumnavigated the world via Cape Horn at the tip of South America. At the time, the longest recorded solo ocean passage was 7,500 miles, sailed by Argentine yachtsman Vito Dumas, from Cape Town to New Zealand during World War II: Chichester's first leg between England and Australia would double this distance. He was also 64 years old and had recently suffered carcinoma of a lung – circumstances that caused a chilling prediction in the *Daily Express* newspaper by clairvoyant Marjorie Staves: "Lone yachtsman Francis Chichester is doomed to failure in his attempt to sail around the world. He will give up due to lack of physical strength."

Chichester's outstanding achievement and ceaseless humour when sailing a boat that he frequently cursed for her "vicious faults" and described as "about as unbalanced or unstable a boat that there could be", inspired a generation of sailors. This tough and resilient yachtsman was not exempt from fear, although it appeared in an unexpected form. On the second leg of the circumnavigation, from Australia to Britain, *Gypsy Moth IV* was hailed by an oil tanker after rounding Cape Horn and heading north-east into the South Atlantic. Chichester's log entry for this incident illustrates the effects of extreme isolation on even the most independent and indomitable spirit: "To my disgust I found that this first contact with people was making me tremble… three months' solitude is strong medicine."

above *Chichester was assisted by hand-pumped Whitbread beer during his round-the-world voyage on board* Gypsy Moth IV. *Spotted loading supplies of gin on to the yacht before setting off on from Plymouth, he commented: "Any damn fool can navigate the world sober. It takes a really good sailor to do it drunk."*

opposite Gypsy Moth IV *rounds Cape Horn in 1967 during a gale. Sir Francis Chichester was amazed – and annoyed – at the presence of the Royal Navy ice patrol ship,* HMS Protector *at the Horn: "I cursed* Protector *for hanging about, especially as I noted that she looked steady enough to play a game of billiards on her deck."* (*from* Gypsy Moth Circles The World*)*

Full rig, smoking [jacket],
smart new trousers, black shoes etc.
the only slip-up is that I left
my bow-tie behind.

Sir Francis Chichester's log on
Gypsy Moth IV records dressing for
dinner on his 65th birthday in
the Doldrums after twenty-one
days alone at sea

The Golden Globe

On 20 July 1969, Neil Armstrong and 'Buzz' Aldrin became the first men to walk on the Moon. The two astronauts spent a total of twenty-one hours on the Moon's surface collecting rock samples and transmitting images and audio back to Earth. A year earlier, nine men set off to race non-stop, single-handed around the planet using navigation techniques that had changed little since the eighteenth-century voyages of Captain James Cook. In an era before GPS (Global Positioning System) and the wide range of meteorological information that is currently available via fax, radio and satellite, the sailors in the 1968 Golden Globe Race represent the purest form of ocean racing.

While modern ocean racers can speak with their families, shore teams or the media on satellite phones and are constantly tracked by Argos beacons installed on board, Knox-Johnston and his fellow yachtsmen depended on unreliable radio sets with patchy coverage for communication and human contact. The absence of satellite tracking and infrequent – or non-existent – radio communication with the competitors meant that the yachtsmen were effectively 'invisible' for extended periods. Often their location and existence was only revealed through chance sightings by deep-sea fishermen or commercial vessels sailing the ocean's shipping lanes. This isolation and information vacuum had a number of consequences: those onshore following the race could only guess whether the sailors were alive, the competitors had no idea where their opponents were and, finally, the situation provided an opportunity for foul play.

The Golden Globe is an important milestone in ocean racing and the same conditions and problems faced by the nine pioneering yachtsmen still affect modern sailors. A brief study of the characters and their experiences during this race demonstrates that solo sailing has always been the most extreme section of the sport:

In 1966, a pair of British soldiers rowed across the Atlantic in a 20ft open boat; two years later, the two men, John Ridgway and Chay Blyth, entered the Golden Globe. Both Ridgway and Blyth sailed twin-keeled, 30ft sloops designed for coastal cruising and were unsuited to ocean racing. Ridgway's *English Rose IV* began to develop serious structural problems in the Atlantic Ocean, forcing an early retirement to the port of Recife, Brazil. With no previous sailing experience, Blyth sailed *Dysticus III* south through the North Atlantic and across the Equator before his self-steering gear failed. After discovering that his fuel supply had been contaminated with seawater, Blyth headed for the island of Tristan da Cunha in the middle of the South Atlantic and received assistance from a fuel tanker anchored off the remote settlement. Noting in his log: "It was my voyage of discovery, and what I discovered was me," Blyth headed for South Africa and retired from the race.

The former British submarine commander Bill King built the 42ft, junk-rigged schooner, *Galway Blazer II*, specifically for a circumnavigation, but a knock-down and total inversion in mid-Atlantic damaged her masts and King sailed to Cape Town and out of the race. The experienced Italian solo sailor Alex Carazzo built 66ft *Gancia Americano* for long distance solo sailing, but stomach ulcer problems and continuously vomiting blood as he sailed through the Bay of Biscay forced Carazzo to retire to Portugal. French yachtsman Loïck Fougeron sailed to the Cape Verde Islands and handed his flea-ridden cat to a local fisherman after she ate through electric cables on board 30ft *Capitaine Browne*. Continuing south, Fougeron was caught in a severe gale and decided to head for Cape Town and retire from the Golden Globe.

The strangest story from the race concerns the British electronics engineer Donald Crowhurst and *Teignmouth Electron*. Crowhurst sailed his 40ft plywood trimaran across the Atlantic towards Brazil, frequently telegraphing record-breaking daily runs and high speeds in Morse code to the race organisation. However, *Teignmouth Electron* did not leave the Atlantic, although her skipper regularly sent radio messages claiming positions throughout the Southern Ocean and even duplicated a false log book plotting his course around the world. After calling into a Brazilian port to make repairs, Crowhurst headed towards England and the finish line, but his deteriorating mental state drove him to suicide in the mid-Atlantic: *Teignmouth Electron* was found drifting in calm seas by a freighter. One of the final entries in Crowhurst's log gives a good indication of his disturbed state of mind:

"my great god who has
revealed at last to his son
not only the exact nature
of his reason for games but
has also revealed the truth of
the way of the ending of the
next game that

It is finished-
It is finished

IT IS THE MERCY"

Sailing a nearly identical trimaran to Crowhurst's, the Royal Navy officer Nigel Tetley succeeded in sailing *Victress* through the world's most fearsome oceans and into the Atlantic. Heading through the North Atlantic towards England, disaster struck when the bow of the multihull's port float fell off. Although a watertight bulkhead prevented the float from filling with water, the detached section had smashed the centre hull's

84

bow and water was pouring into the yacht. Tetley grabbed the radio: "Mayday, Mayday, Mayday. This is sailing yacht *Victress* at Latitude 39° 10' North, Longitude 24° 30' West. I am sinking and require assistance. Mayday, Mayday, Mayday." A Dutch ship immediately replied and Tetley climbed into his liferaft as *Victress* sank to the bottom.

The inspiration to compete in such a dangerous, physically and mentally demanding event differed for all the competitors. 28-year-old British Merchant Marine captain Robin Knox-Johnston was driven by adventure, patriotism and admiration for the circumnavigation of Sir Francis Chichester, saying: "Once Chichester had shown that this trip was possible, I could not accept that anyone but a Briton should be the first to do it, and I wanted to be that Briton." The stimulation for 45-year-old French yachtsman and author, Bernard Moitessier, is less distinct, but resembles the desires of Alain Gerbault and his search for personal freedom. Moitessier, however, was vocal in his dislike for the 'civilized' world and raged in his log book against its "false gods, always lying in wait, spider-like, eating our liver, sucking our marrow."

While Knox-Johnston battled through the Southern Ocean on his solid teak 32ft ketch *Suhaili*, Moitessier wrestled with his personal demons and a consuming love affair with nature on board 39ft steel-hulled *Joshua*. Passing Cape Horn, Knox-Johnston scrawled "Yippee!!!" in his log book and celebrated the momentous occasion by unwrapping his Aunt Aileen's fruitcake, while – chasing hard – Moitessier was moved to poetic prose: "*Joshua* drives towards the Horn under the light of the stars and the somewhat distant tenderness of the moon… I no longer know how far I have got, except that we long ago left the borders of too much behind." Entering the Atlantic was a defining moment for Moitessier and as Knox-Johnston continued north-east towards the finish line and victory, the mystical Frenchman turned south-east to the tip of South Africa and into the Indian Ocean. Off Cape Town, *Joshua* sailed close to a British oil tanker and Moitessier used his handheld catapult to shoot a final message on to the ship's deck: "My intention is to continue the voyage, still non-stop, towards the Pacific Islands, where there is plenty of sun and more peace than Europe."

I am continuing non-stop because I am happy at sea and perhaps because I want to save my soul.

Bernard Moitessier's final message to the Golden Globe race organisation

6

Offshore Solo

- THE OSTAR

- THE TRANSAT

- ROUTE DU RHUM

- THE FIGARO

- MINI TRANSAT
  (TRANSAT 6.50)

The OSTAR

In 1960 four Britons and one Frenchman raced single-handed from Plymouth, England, to New York for a 'Half Crown' wager (approx. twenty-five pence) and the OSTAR (*Observer* Single-handed Transatlantic Race) was born. Organized by the Royal Western Yacht Club in Plymouth and held every four years, the race is open to professional and amateur sailors in a variety of boat sizes, both monohulls and multihulls. Today, the race still maintains its 'Corinthian' element and legendary status, attracting sailors from around the world to an event known as 'La Transat Anglaise'.

Although the spirit of the first OSTAR remains, the race has undergone many name and rule changes throughout its history, including moving the finish from New York to Newport, Rhode Island. What remains unaltered, however, is the ferocious attrition rate as the racing fleet heads west into the Atlantic. The event's history is littered with sinking or abandoned yachts and courageous rescue and salvage attempts. Possibly the most astonishing tale from the OSTAR concerns the sinking of the 30ft monohull *Hyccup* after an attack by whales in 1988. The yacht's skipper, David Sellings, climbed into a liferaft and was spotted by a Nimrod aeroplane. Later, via radio from the rescue ship, Sellings recounted the experience:

"On the first night, I saw several whales in the distance. The next night I heard them grunting and squealing like pigs in a trough. They were clearly talking to each other and bringing other whales in. They went away and came back next morning. This time there were more of them, probably fifty or sixty, they kept coming closer, making an awful lot of noise and pushing tight up against the boat. There were two distinct bumps and that was it. The rudder was smashed and they had disabled the ship."

Although the sinking of *Hyccup* is sinister and unique, the retirement rate has hovered around the 50 per cent level for the past two editions. Further patterns that reflect the development of solo sailing emerge from the results of the OSTAR: the French dominance of the sport and a period of dramatic advances in boat design. These improvements and the introduction of professional offshore sailors saw the transatlantic race time slip below twenty days and then fall below the ten-day barrier by 2000. During the 1976 OSTAR, 42 per cent of the racing fleet was forced to retire and two skippers were lost: this tragedy generated a focus on safety measures and the casualty rate subsequently dropped while the yachts continued to slash days from the OSTAR race record. Finally, the retirement rate from the most recent OSTAR in 2005 is identical to the attrition percentage during the 1968 edition of the race and indicates a return to the event's 'Corinthian' roots with the participation of adventurous, amateur sailors.

Q: What caused you to retire?

A: Knocked down in Force 11, thrown overboard, harness held, injured shoulder, torn main, torn jib, main compass broken, all electronic instruments out, batteries lost acid, VHF gone.

Q: By whom were you rescued?

A: Made port under own steam.

Colin Drummond, skipper of *Sleuth Hound*, in his retirement questionnaire form after the 1976 OSTAR

previous page *French trimaran ace Loïck Peyron flies off the start line of the 2002 Route du Rhum on* Fujicolor. *Huge seas and high winds devastated the ORMA 60 trimaran fleet forcing a majority of the yachts to retire. Peyron's multihull began to break up as he drove hard into the North Atlantic.*

above *Sir Francis Chichester leans against the mast of* Gypsy Moth III *shortly before the start of the 1964 OSTAR discussing tactics with the only French entrant, a naval lieutenant, Eric Tabarly (far right). Chichester had won the inaugural OSTAR four years earlier taking 40 days to cross the Atlantic: Tabarly won the 1964 race in just 27 days aboard his 44ft ketch,* Pen Duick II. *Having crossed the finish line, Tabarly let slip that his self steering gear had failed after eight days at sea. President de Gaulle awarded the new French sailing legend with the Legion of Honour.*

The OSTAR roll of honour and casualty list 1960-2005:

1960 OSTAR (Plymouth-New York)
Winner: Sir Francis Chichester (GBR) *Gypsy Moth III*
Time: 40d 12h 30m
Total of 5 competitors at the start. 100% of fleet finishes the race

1964 OSTAR (Plymouth-Newport, Rhode Island)
Winner: Eric Tabarly (FRA) *Pen Duick II*
Time: 27d 03h 56m
Total of 15 competitors at the start. 93% of fleet finish the race
Details: 1 yacht retires

1968 OSTAR
Winner (monohull): Geoffrey Williams (GBR) *Sir Thomas Lipton*
Time: 25d 20h 33m
Winner (multihull): Bill Howell (AUS) *Golden Cockerel*
Time: 31d 16h 24m
Total of 35 competitors at the start. 51% of the fleet finish the race
Details: 1 yacht disqualified, 12 retire, 4 abandoned or sunk

1972 OSTAR
Winner (multihull): Alain Colas (FRA) *Pen Duick IV*
Time: 20d 13h 15m
Winner (monohull): Jean-Yves Terlain (FRA) *Vendredi Treize*
Time: 21d 05h 14m
Total of 55 competitors at the start. 72% of the fleet finish the race
Details: 10 yachts retire, 1 abandoned

1976 OSTAR
Winner (monohull): Eric Tabarly (FRA) *Pen Duick VI*
Time: 23d 20h 12m
Winner (multihull): Mike Birch (Canada) *The Third Turtle*
Time: 24d 20h 39m
Total of 125 competitors at the start. 58% of the fleet complete the race
Details: 40 yachts retired, 6 abandoned or sunk, 5 finish outside the race time limit, 2 skippers lost

1980 OSTAR
Winner (multihull): Philip Weld (USA) *Moxie*
Time: 17d 23h 12m
Winner (monohull): Kazimierz Jaworski (Poland) *Spaniel II*
Time: 19d 13h 25m
Total of 90 competitors at the start. 80% of the fleet complete the race
Details: 4 yachts abandoned or sunk, 12 retire, 1 disqualified

1984 Carlsberg
Winner (trimaran): Yvon Fauconier (FRA) *Umupro Jardin V*
Time: 16d 22h 25m
Winner (catamaran): Marc Pajot (FRA) *Elf Aquitaine II*
Time: 16d 12h 18m
Winner (monohull): Warren Luhrs (USA) *Thursday's Child*
Time: 16d 22h 27m
Total of 91 competitors at the start. 70% of the fleet complete the race
Details: 19 yachts retire, 8 sunk or abandoned

1988 Carlsberg
Winner (trimaran): Philippe Poupon (FRA) *Fleury Michon*
Time: 10d 09h 15m
Winner (catamaran): Bruno Peyron (FRA) *VSD*
Time: 12d 23h 20m
Winner (monohull): Jean Yves Terlain (FRA) *UAP 1992*
Time: 17d 04h 05m
Total of 95 competitors at the start. 76% of the fleet complete the race
Details: 17 yachts retire, 5 sunk or abandoned

1992 Europe 1 Star
Winner (multihull): Loïck Peyron (FRA) *Fujicolor*
Time: 11d 01h 35m
Winner (monohull): Yves Parlier (FRA) *Cacolac d'Aquitaine*
Time: 14d 16h 01m
Total of 66 competitors at the start. 83% of the fleet complete the race
Details: 3 skippers retire through injury or fatigue, 1 dismasting, 1 capsize, 1 collision with debris

1996 Europe 1 Star
Winner (multihull): Loïck Peyron (FRA) *Fujicolor II*
Time: 10d 10h 05m
Winner (monohull): Gerry Roufs (FRA) *Groupe LG2*
Time: 15d 14h 50m
Total of 69 competitors. 56% of the fleet complete the race
Details:

2000 Europe 1 New Man Star
Winner (trimaran): Francis Joyon (FRA) *Eure et Loire*
Time: 09d 23h 21m
Winner (monohull): Ellen MacArthur (GBR) *Kingfisher*
Time: 14d 23h 01m
Total of 69 competitors. 56% of the fleet complete the race
Details: 4 yachts dismasted, 3 retire with associated mast problems, 4 retire with autopilot and self steering gear failure

2005 Faraday Mill OSTAR
Winner (multihull): Franco Manzoli (ITA) *Cotonella*
Time: 17d 21h 41m
Winner (monohull): Steve White (GBR) *Olympian Challenger*
Time: 20d 5h 24m
Total of 35 competitors. 51% of the fleet complete the race
Details: 1 dismasting, 1 retires with injured skipper, and 15 retire with rigging and equipment failure

previous page *Italian solo sailor Giovanni Soldini straps into the starboard helm pod on* TIM *during the 2002 Route du Rhum. Solo trimaran skippers cannot risk leaving the tiller in rough conditions and may be forced to* steer the boat for extended periods denying the yachtsmen any rest or the ability to eat cooked food.

above *British 60ft monohull skipper Mike Golding "fried" the electronic motor*

The Transat

Organized by the professional racing team Offshore Challenges Events, The Transat 2004 provided a North Atlantic 'sprint' for 50- and 60-foot monohulls and multihulls between Plymouth, England, and Boston, Massachusetts. On 31 May, thirty-seven solo sailors crossed the start line off Penlee Point in blustery and rough conditions that were to continue for the majority of the 2,800-mile course. The early stages of the race along the southern coast of England were brutal: 20-knot headwinds forced constant tacking and manoeuvring within the tightly packed fleet preventing skippers from snatching any rest during their first night at sea.

As the second North Atlantic depression began gathering size and momentum to the west of the fleet, a period of light winds and thick fog hampered progress. This period of light, shifting breeze demanded constant sail trimming and lowered the morale of many skippers already exhausted by three days of beating to windward. The predicted 35-knot winds rolling eastwards were preceded by confused seas and the majority of the racing fleet headed north to avoid the headwinds on the bottom edge of the depression spinning anti-clockwise towards them. Timing the weather system's progress would be crucial for the leading multihulls; judging the exact moment to bear away south-west from the centre of the depression to sail fast downwind was a key moment of the race.

All of the ORMA 60 trimaran fleet escaped from the high winds of the low pressure system without capsizing, but not without incident. Alain Gautier, skipper of *Foncia*, described passing through the eye of the storm on his satellite phone: "The night was hard when we passed the centre of the low pressure with rough sea and wind increasing to around 45 or 50 knots. I was on starboard [tack] for one hour and, suddenly, in two minutes it was Armageddon – the mainsheet broke and the boom flew out, breaking four of the battens. I have to drop the mainsail, but in 45 knots… it's not easy."

The 60ft monohull fleet was not so fortunate. Sailing under storm-jib only, Jean-Pierre Dick and Open 60 monohull *Virbac* rolled through 360° in 50-knot winds and 6–7m waves approximately 100 miles from the centre of the depression. Dick was down below when the yacht rolled and survived uninjured, but the yacht's mast was broken in three places. With the structural integrity of the hull intact, the French

powering his yacht's canting keel mechanism in the opening hours of The Transat 2004. Many skippers would have retired from racing before entering the fierce North Atlantic weather ahead, but Golding chose to continue. For 2,800 miles

he used a perilous method of overpowering Ecover *and "laying her on her ear" to drop the keel to leeward. Golding could then tack the boat leaving the keel on the windward side. His plan succeeded and* Ecover *took monohull line honours.*

skipper declined any offers of outside assistance from other competitors and began constructing a jury rig from the stump of his mast. Three days later, the 60ft monohull *PRB*, skippered by Vincent Riou, dismasted and two hours later – sixty miles to the north-west – Franco–Swiss skipper Bernard Stamm activated his distress beacon when the keel detached from his 60ft monohull *Cheminees Poujoulat-Armor Lux*, 360 miles west of St. Johns, Newfoundland. All three yachts and skippers involved in the mid-Atlantic catastrophe survived: Stamm was rescued from his upturned hull by the crew of a small tanker and later salvaged his yacht with an ocean-going tug based in Newfoundland, while Riou, Dick and their yachts were towed back to France.

High drama continued as yachts approached the American coast. Thick fog, fishing vessels, icebergs and drilling platforms in the Flemish Cap and Grand Banks areas off Newfoundland proved a hazard for the fleet. The most dramatic incident occurred on *Sodebo*, the ORMA 60 trimaran skippered by Thomas Coville. Travelling at 22–23 knots in a wind building to 35 knots, Coville was preparing to take in his third reef when the boat collided with something. Winching in the reef and facing aft to protect himself from constant spray, Coville was catapulted across the cockpit and knocked unconscious. The French skipper called the race organization after regaining consciousness: "I do not know how long I was unconscious for. It might have been seconds or a few minutes.

above *Thomas Coville was knocked unconscious on* Sodebo *during the single-handed Transat 2004 when a whale became wedged between the daggerboard and rudder of the 60ft trimaran's starboard float. Collisions with whales and debris cause a dramatic number of retirements in offshore racing. Coville recovered to take second place in the ORMA multihull class.*

opposite *The ORMA 60 fleet start The Transat 2004 heavily reefed due to the squalls and boat-breaking seas off Plymouth. After the first night of racing, Michel Desjoyeaux on trimaran,* Géant, *declared: "I'm too old to take all these waves". Nonetheless, Desjoyeaux led the multihull fleet through the North Atlantic, taking line honours in Boston.*

> # Every wave made me cringe as the ear-splitting sound of carbon slamming against the ocean was taking its toll.
>
> Conrad Humphreys, skipper of *Hellomoto*, feels the effects of a mid-Atlantic depression during The Transat 2004

I couldn't see or hear anything. Then there was a sound and a sharp pain in my temple, which made me look around. I could see the boat was in good shape and the mast too. I stood up and touched my head… thankfully I had been wearing my survival suit and its neoprene hood protected me."

Having confirmed that he was uninjured, Coville wanted to investigate the condition of *Sodebo* and discover what had caused the impact: "The boat had stopped… or nearly. I took a light to check the daggerboard… for me the race seemed over. In the fluorescent part of the water I could see a large white object around the daggerboard. I dropped the mainsail and the jib and lifted the daggerboard beyond its normal limit with a halyard. As I did this, I felt the boat break free and we were off again." Trapping a whale – if it was a whale – between the daggerboard and rudder failed to stop Coville continuing the race and finishing in 2nd place, just two hours behind winner Michel Desjoyeaux on *Géant*.

Racing was equally close at the head of the IMOCA 60 monohull fleet. Hampered by the failure of his canting keel's hydraulic motor within hours of the start, Mike Golding on *Ecover* finished 1st, beating Swiss skipper Dominique Wavre on *Temenos* in 2nd, and New Zealand's Mike Sanderson on *Pindar Alphagraphics* in 3rd. The trio had stayed within thirty miles of each other for the final 1,400 miles of racing.

Route du Rhum

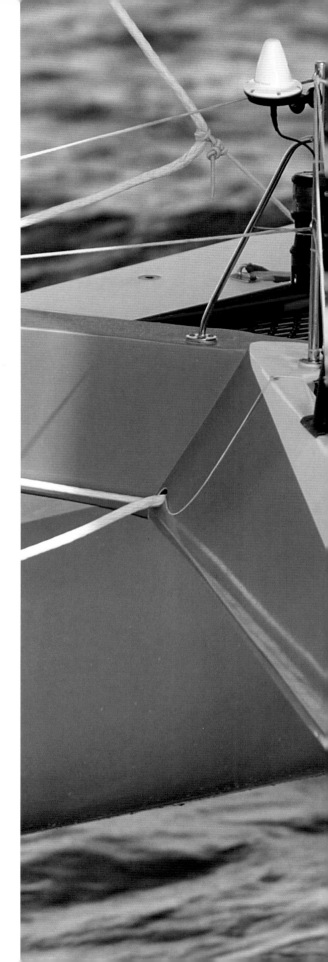

Covering 3,600 miles from the French port of St Malo to Point-à-Pitre, Guadeloupe, in the eastern Caribbean and raced by monohulls and multihulls, the Route du Rhum is arguably the toughest, most demanding single-handed transatlantic event. Held every four years since the inaugural race in 1978 and originally created to challenge the British-run OSTAR, the 'Rhum' attracts solo sailing's elite and produces extraordinary levels of competition between participants. The race has also yielded two outstanding female victories in what is a male-dominated area of offshore sailing. French yachtswoman, Florence Arthaud, won the 1990 edition of the race and Britain's Ellen MacArthur took line honours in 2002, becoming the first monohull sailor to beat the Route du Rhum's multihull fleet.

The 2002 Route du Rhum will always be remembered for the catastrophic disaster rate in the ORMA 60 fleet as fifteen of the original eighteen multihulls entered in the race either capsized or suffered damage that forced retirement. Although none of the skippers were lost overboard, the 2002 edition of the race illustrated that pushing a trimaran hard on the limit of control is highly dangerous. Only the skill of the sailors involved and the strength of their boats averted tragedy. Starting a Northern Hemisphere race in the stormy conditions usually experienced in November adds to the risks involved. Consequently, the 2006 Route du Rhum is scheduled to start in October.

A timeline of the 2002 Route du Rhum's multihull victor, Michel Desjoyeaux of France, demonstrates why 'Le Professeur' is possibly the world's ultimate solo sailor:

November 10: Eighteen 60ft trimarans cross the start line off St Malo.

November 11: Desjoyeaux makes a three-hour pit stop in a bay outside Brest harbour to rectify autopilot problems on *Géant* and repair broken mainsail battens.

November 12: To avoid a deep depression, Desjoyeaux heads west to keep above the weather system. While many in the trimaran fleet suffer 80 knots of wind, *Géant* records wind speeds of 40–45 knots.

November 13: Desjoyeaux sails through a second depression under bare poles (no sails).

November 15: On hearing reports that two trimarans similar to *Géant* have suffered wave impact damage to the forward beams connecting their hulls, Desjoyeaux rendezvous with this shore team on the island of Porto Santo, north-east of Madeira. After a 15-hour stop over for repairs, the multihull leaves port and continues racing.

November 19: Leading the remaining four trimarans, Steve Ravussin capsizes *Technomarine* and Desjoyeaux takes pole position. The French skipper remarks: "I have been parachuted into the lead by the misfortune of others. This is maybe not ideal."

November 23: *Géant* crosses the finish line after 13 days and 8 hours' racing. Desjoyeaux completed the race at an average speed of 14.2 knots.

Sailing a monohull single-handed, you are racing. Sailing a trimaran single-handed, you are risking your life.

Loïck Peyron,

solo trimaran skipper

left *British skipper Sam Davies, on the 32ft Figaro Beneteau Skandia, was one of only three women competing in a fleet of 46 boats during the 2005 Solitaire Afflelou Le Figaro. Raced in identical yachts, The Figaro is a demanding mix of inshore and offshore solo sailing with stop over ports in France, Spain and Ireland. Close racing and constant sail trimming causes extreme levels of sleep deprivation among skippers.*

The Figaro

previous page *Michel Desjoyeaux crosses the single-handed transatlantic 2002 Route du Rhum finish line off Guadeloupe on ORMA 60 trimaran,* Géant. *The protective screen around the helming pod provides vital protection from spray constantly flying aft through the trampoline netting strung between the yacht's hull and floats. Desjoyeaux's multihull victory in the 2002 Route du Rhum and his earlier monohull win in the 2000–01 Vendée Globe were followed by trimaran triumph in the 2004 Transat as "Le Professeur" claimed the laurels for solo sailing's 'big three'.*

below *French skipper Jérémie Beyou won the final leg of the Solitaire Afflelou Le Figaro on* Delta Dore *sailing from Cork in southern Ireland to Port Bourgenay, France. Beyou took 51 hours to sail 496 miles alone across some of the busiest shipping lanes in the world. This victory clinched an overall win for the 1,460-mile race.*

The annual Figaro season of offshore solo races is a proving ground for aspiring single-handed sailors. The race series provides a balance between inshore and offshore racing and has been dominated by French solo sailors since the inaugural race in 1970. A list of Figaro victors reveals the pedigree of sailing talent required to win this race: Christophe Augin (1986), Laurent Bourgnon (1988), Jean Le Cam (1994, 1996 and 1999), Alain Gautier (1989) and Michel Desjoyeaux (1992 and 1998).

The 2005 edition of the race involved four separate legs raced between ports in France, Spain and Ireland covering just less than 1,500 miles at sea. Racing identical 32ft yachts, the skippers are forbidden satellite communication systems and must rely on weather information from faxes and radio broadcasts. The communications ban includes satellite phones and competitors can only converse via VHF. The Figaro is raced through the busiest commercial shipping lanes in the world along the Bay of Biscay and across the English Channel: this feature adds to the sleep deprivation experienced by skippers already racing hard and close in a tightly packed fleet.

inset left *French skipper, Sebastien Gladu, prepares supper on Transat 6.50, Armor Lux. In addition to 100 litres of water and 35 kilos of food, the cramped interior must serve as storage for the yacht's sails, a liferaft, medical supplies, spare parts and the small amount of electronics carried onboard a Mini Transat yacht. A bucket serves as both bathroom and washroom.*

Mini Transat

The Transat 6.50 is the smallest boat in the 'Open' class with a reputation for radical, fast designs demanding endurance and nerves of steel from their skippers. The class was an English innovation as a cheap alternative to the single-handed OSTAR race where bigger boats required budgets and sponsorship deals unavailable to solo sailors trying to break into the sport. Today, the Mini Transat racing circuit is a predominantly French event, although well funded projects from outside France are re-establishing a foothold within the class.

The Mini fleet is divided into two sub-sections; 'protos' (custom-built boats) and 'series' (production models), but both the categories are very similar in size. During the longest race in the Mini calendar, skippers will spend around twenty-eight days in the Atlantic on a boat that is no bigger than an inshore dinghy. The conditions on board are minimalist and cramped in a racing machine that is designed for speed, with no concessions for comfort. The sail area on a Mini is out of proportion with the boat's size: the mast is a little under twice the length of the hull and a three-metre bowsprit almost doubles the length of the boat, enabling a sail area of around 100 square metres. Recent designs incorporate a bowsprit that swivels around a fitting on the yacht's stem, allowing the spar to be swung out from the boat like a switchblade. Wisely, the class organisation has forbidden their use on the start line and the long poles must be stowed inboard to prevent any carnage in the early stages of a race.

Mini Transat boats are an example of high technology applied to the purest form of solo sailing. While the class is seen as a testing ground for new designs, the skippers are allowed only a few relatively low-tech gadgets onboard. An autopilot is obviously a fundamental requirement and this self-steering system is powered by solar panels. These vital screens are usually mounted on brackets over the stern to limit the risk of damage and reduce any potential power loss through shadows cast by the sails. The yachts are allowed GPS to aid navigation, but Internet communication is forbidden. Although weather information can be received by long-range SSB radio, the skippers are not permitted to transmit on this equipment and all voice communication is limited to short-range VHF radio. This ocean racing communications blackout is unique to the Mini class and skippers on bigger, 40–60ft 'Open' boats can maintain contact with family and shore teams via satellite phones and email. After a transatlantic Mini race, it is difficult to stop the skippers from talking once they have crossed the finish line and post-race press conferences are often the liveliest in the sport.

above *It takes approximately four paces to walk from bow to stern on a Transat 6.50. For four weeks during the Mini Transat race from La Rochelle, France, to Salvador de Bahia in Brazil, this dinghy-sized, offshore rocket is home. The skippers are only allowed to transmit on short-range VHF radio, and apart from a brief stop over at Lanzarote in the Canary Islands, contact with the outside world is minimal.*

7

Solo
Round
The
World
Races

- THE VENDÉE GLOBE

- VELUX 5 OCEANS RACE

The Vendée Globe

The concept of the Vendée Globe is simple: sail around the world alone, non-stop, without any outside assistance. In reality, the race is arguably the toughest sporting challenge known to man. Held every four years, the event is based in the town of Les Sables d'Olonne on the Bay of Biscay in the Vendée region of France and attracts the world's solo sailing elite.

After the 2000–01 edition of the Vendée Globe, entry was limited to Open 60 yachts: high-tech, super-light, carbon fibre racing machines using the latest developments in boat design and manufacture. Sailing skill and owning a fast, new yacht are not enough to successfully complete this race: impeccable boat preparation, self-motivation, endurance and courage are required to survive the hostile environment of the Southern Ocean and the relentless racing pace of the 23,000-mile circumnavigation.

A key feature of the Vendée Globe is the rule forbidding outside assistance. This removes the opportunity for a competitor to receive aid or materials from a third party, effectively preventing a skipper from docking alongside a quay or another vessel and obtaining spare parts dropped from ships or aircraft. For this reason, a skipper must be talented in all aspects of boat management. Being an accomplished sailor, navigator and meteorologist is insufficient – a skipper must possess the ability to operate as boatbuilder, plumber, electrician, rigger and sailmaker.

Every edition of the race is rich with stories of extraordinary willpower, but the dogged determination to nurse a damaged yacht around the world is typified by French yachtsman, Jean-Pierre Dick in 2004–05:

Just eleven days into the race, his yacht, *Virbac-Paprec*, developed problems with the vital gooseneck fitting connecting the boom to the mast. The following day, J-P Dick was forced to dive under the boat and remove a long length of line and debris from around the yacht's keel. Then, shortly after crossing the Equator, a lashing on the gennaker tack failed. As the huge headsail thrashed around in strong winds, it ripped the stainless steel pulpit from the foredeck leaving large holes and a vital repair project for the skipper. Heading into the Indian Ocean, the engine failed leaving Dick unable to charge the batteries and run the vital electronic systems and autopilot. Deciding to rely on solar panels for electricity, the skipper chose to continue racing with the prospect of hand steering for six or seven hours at a time. Running under reduced power, the autopilot became unable to steer in heavy conditions and the boat broached, burying her boom underwater and breaking the gooseneck fitting. After sixty-one days at sea, the yacht's boom broke in the depths of the Southern Ocean, 1,200 miles west of Cape Horn. Dick made temporary repairs and rounded the world's southernmost cape six days later. In the South Atlantic he completed the boom repairs and made a final dive below the boat to remove a huge bed of kelp wrapped around the keel before finishing the race in 6th place after ninety-eight days at sea.

previous page *American skipper Brad van Liew won every leg of the 2002–03 Around Alone for Class II on Open 50,* Tommy Hilfiger-Freedom America. *Pictured off Tauranga, New Zealand, van Liew deploys his asymmetric spinnaker: on many solo sailing yachts the spinnaker is hauled up the mast in a 'sock' that is then lifted allowing the sail to fill. The spinnaker can be quickly 'snuffed' by pulling the sock downwards over the sail… in theory.*

opposite *Michel Desjoyeaux won the 2000–01 Vendée Globe taking 90 days to race Open 60,* PRB, *around the planet. After crossing the finishing line, "Le Professeur" reflected on the race: "This single-handed trip around the world is an incredible page in your life history: it adds years to your age, it makes you more mature and throws things into perspective."*

next page left *Engine failure on board Jean-Pierre Dick's Open 60,* Virbac, *in the Indian Ocean left the French skipper with no method of charging his batteries to run the yacht's electrical systems. Dick chose to continue racing using the power generated by solar panels to run the vital autopilot. Sailing with a dramatically reduced power supply, Dick was forced to hand steer for 6–7 hours at a time for over half the 2004–05 Vendée Globe circumnavigation.*

One cannot come home from a Vendée Globe without bearing any marks. Several months will undoubtedly be necessary for me to come back to my normal life ashore. The Deep South let me through this time. The real enemy in this voyage is firstly the sea itself.

Christophe Auguin, French winner of the 1996–97 Vendée Globe

The good thing about spending New Year's Eve in the middle of the ocean is that the cops can't chuck me in jail

Australian skipper, Nick Moloney, prepares for celebrations on
Open 60 Skandia during the 2004–05 Vendée Globe

Ellen MacArthur shot into the global limelight after finishing 2nd in the 2000–01 Vendée Globe, crossing the finish line off Les Sables d'Olonne, France, 24 hours after race winner, Michel Desjoyeaux. Her achievement stunned the offshore racing community and merited one of the highest accolades in solo sailing – a nickname – 'La Petite Anglaise'.

Since the first edition of the Vendée Globe in 1989–90, the event has been filled with drama and extraordinary examples of seamanship. In 1992, the first Briton to enter the race, Nigel Burgess, was found drowned off Cape Finisterre just four days after the start when gales forced many skippers to return to Les Sables d'Olonne with damaged boats. During the 1996–97 race, Raphaël Dinelli was plucked from his liferaft by British sailor Pete Goss after the Frenchman's yacht, *Algimouss*, capsized in the Southern Ocean. In the same patch of ocean, Thierry Dubois from France and English yachtsman Tony Bullimore were pulled from their stricken yachts by the Australian Navy. Another Vendée tragedy of the same year was the loss of Gerry Roufs whose yacht, *Groupe LG*, was found drifting upside down off the coast of Chile, South America, six months after the race organization lost contact with the Canadian sailor.

The following race in 2000–01 produced extreme levels of ingenuity as Yves Parlier single-handedly repaired the broken mast of 60ft Aquitaine *Innovations* while anchored off a Pacific island before continuing to race halfway round the world. Disaster struck Catherine Chabaud late in the same race when *Whirlpool* dismasted as the French yachtswoman approached the continent. In the same year, a young English entrant, Ellen MacArthur, astonished the solo sailing community by finishing in 2nd place.

The recent Vendée Globe in 2004–05 yielded the fastest and most exciting edition of the event as yachts sped round the world breaking all previous race records. Although additional Southern Ocean waypoints were introduced for this edition of the race to keep the fleet north of the predicted ice limit, the yachts flew through a barrier of icebergs and fog between New Zealand and Antarctica at the 'halfway' point in the circumnavigation. The intense competition throughout the fleet and between the leading three boats in particular forced the skippers to push themselves and their yachts to the limit for the entire length of the Pacific and Atlantic Oceans, driving the battered boats hard until the finish line.

above *After 28 days at sea, Open 60, Hellomoto, broke the tip of her starboard rudder on floating debris after a high speed collision in the South Atlantic during the 2004–05 Vendée Globe. Her skipper, Conrad Humphreys, nursed the yacht to a mooring off Simonstown in False Bay near the Cape of Good Hope, South Africa. Without infringing race rules governing assistance by a third party, the British skipper single-handedly replaced the damaged rudder with a spare carried onboard and continued racing.*

109

previous page right *When Mike Golding rounded the Cape of Good Hope, he was 800 miles behind the lead yacht in the 2004–05 Vendée Globe. Thirty-one days later, after 10,000 miles of Southern Ocean racing, the British skipper had reduced this deficit to 113 miles as Ecover rounded Cape Horn. Golding modestly commented: "The boat's the star of the show." A further 7,000 miles later, the keel dropped off the bottom of Golding's yacht within sight of the finish line: he managed to sail the remaining 50 miles taking third place and becoming the first yachtsman to finish an offshore race without a keel.*

Velux 5 Oceans Race

Raced in customized Open 60 and 50 yachts, the single-handed 2006 Velux 5 Oceans race is descended from the 1982–83 BOC (British Oxygen Corporation) Challenge and pre-dates the Vendée Globe by seven years. The race also includes a number of stop-overs – usually three or four – and the yachtsmen are allowed to seek outside assistance and pull into port, although this incurs a time penalty. Many solo sailors believe that the Velux 5 Oceans (ex-BOC Challenge, ex-Around Alone Race) pushes boats harder than in the Vendée Globe as the skippers are able to rely on shore teams patching the yachts back together after they have been thrashed across the oceans.

Certainly, yachts take a beating in the race and the opportunity to seek assistance offshore during the 30,000-mile circumnavigation is often invaluable. In the 2002–03 Around Alone Race, the 60ft yacht *Hexagon* broke her boom in a Pacific Ocean gale and her New Zealand skipper, Graham Dalton, arranged to rendezvous with his shore crew off the coast of Tierra del Fuego, just north-east of Cape Horn. His team repaired the damage and Dalton continued racing although he dismasted a few days later off the coast of Patagonia. During the same race, two yachts diverted to Port Stanley in the Falkland Islands for repair work and one yacht motored into the port of Ushuaia in Argentina having dismasted off Cape Horn.

Although the winner of the first BOC Challenge, Philippe Jeantot, went on to found the non-stop Vendée Globe in a quest for the ultimate solo sailing experience, the 1982–83 race gave a clear, early warning of the dangers inherent in offshore solo sailing. An incident on Leg 3 between Sidney and Rio de Janeiro proved to be a template for a very similar disaster in the Vendée Globe fourteen years later.

In huge following seas the 41ft (12.5m) yacht, *Skoiern III*, pitch-poled violently, burying her bow and instantly dismasting. The yacht's foredeck hatch was ripped from its hinges and icy water poured into the boat at such a rate that the pressure change popped the ears of her French skipper, Jacques de Roux. Bleeding and semi-concussed, the former submariner grabbed his yellow Argos distress transponder, moved the large emergency button to 'transmit' and started pumping water out of the boat.

Pitch-poling a yacht and dismasting is catastrophic when sailing close inshore, but the forward somersault performed by *Skoiern III* took place in the most desolate area of the Pacific Ocean. The French yachtsman was sinking 2,400 miles east of the southern tip of South Island, New Zealand, and 2,200 miles west of Cape Horn. The nearest speck of land was Pitcairn Island, 1,800 miles due north. Two hours after De Roux activated his distress beacon, its signal reached the Argos

above *Josh Hall and Open 60 Gartmore during the single-handed, 1998–99 Around Alone (formerly the 'BOC Challenge' and now the 'Velux 5 Oceans Race'). Stop-over ports during the circumnavigation allow skippers to push their boats hard across the Atlantic, Indian, Pacific and Southern Ocean in the knowledge that a professional shore crew will repair any damage. Sometimes, the boats are pushed too hard: Hall lost his 82ft mast on Leg 3 and diverted to the Chatham Islands, 420 miles due east of Christchurch, New Zealand.*

decoding station in Toulouse, France, and a network of ham radio enthusiasts immediately began the task of contacting the BOC yachts closest to *Skoiern III*. With the nearest commercial shipping lane thousands of miles to the north, it was clear that any rescue attempt would have to be undertaken by fellow competitors. After twelve hours of constant calling, a radio ham reached 52ft (15.65m) *Perseverance of Medina*, skippered by British yachtsman, Richard Broadhead, positioned approximately 300 miles east of *Skoiern III*. Broadhead turned his yacht around and headed into the wind and huge seas, making only 5 knots of boat speed and hampered by thick fog.

Forty-seven hours after being alerted, Broadhead arrived at the Argos position of *Skoiern III*, but there was no sign of the yacht. Could De Roux have survived for three days? The British skipper went below to radio for a position check, unaware that the dismasted yacht was only 50 yards away, hidden behind a tall swell rolling down from the west. De Roux, however, had spotted *Perseverance* and leapt about on deck shouting and waving his arms and let off seven flares to attract Broadhead's attention although his rescuer was already below decks concentrating on his radio set. Hours later, Broadhead reappeared from below and his eyes were caught by a white flash two miles away: a

above left *Thierry Dubois, displays complete faith in his autopilot as he charges into Salvador de Bahia, Brazil, on* Solidaire *at the finish of Leg 4 during the 2002–03 Around Alone. Light winds and slow progress frustrated Dubois as he approached the Brazilian coastline and the French skipper set fire to a stuffed toy of a kiwi – a souvenir from the New Zealand stop over – in a desperate sacrifice to the wind gods. The race organisation became alarmed when Dubois threatened to shoot himself unless the wind increased: fortunately,* Solidaire *carries no firearms.*

above right *Franco-Swiss skipper, Bernard Stamm, took Class 1 (60ft) line honours on every leg of the 2002–03 Around Alone and consistently sailed* Bobst Group-Armor Lux *with the throttle wide open, whatever the sea conditions. Stamm arrived in New Zealand at the finish of Leg 3 with a six-foot section of carbon fibre peeling from the starboard side of his hull after crossing the Indian Ocean. On the following leg to Brazil, he was forced to make a swift pit stop at Port Stanley in the Falkland Islands to repair damage to the yacht's keel after rounding Cape Horn.*

scrap of sail on the French yacht's stump of a mast. In building seas the transfer was difficult and the two yachts collided a number of times before De Roux leapt from the deck of *Skoiern III* as Broadhead made his fourth pass, mistiming the jump but managing to grab the guardrails as *Perseverance* rolled away from the sinking yacht. Broadhead describes the scene:

"He was absolutely knackered. He just hung there by his armpits over the top of the lifelines and if the two boats had come together again, he would have lost his legs."

Four hours after the rescue, De Roux's Argos beacon ceased sending a signal: *Skoiern III* had sunk in 4,000 metres of freezing water. Three days later, *Perseverance* made a mid-ocean rendezvous with a French Navy ship and De Roux was transferred aboard in exchange for a hamper of food and a plentiful supply of wine.

8

For The Record

How to break a sailing record

The diversity within sailing provides the World Sailing Speed Record Council (WSSRC) with a complex task. Record attempts are sub-divided by three main factors: 1) the type of yacht, 2) the number of crew, 3) the distance covered.

1 The enormous variety of yachts attempting to break records produces a long menu of options: IMS (International Measurement System), IOR (International Offshore Rule), ULDB (Ultra Light Displacement Yachts), trimarans, catamarans, monohulls, etc. A separate division is provided for "a vessel with powered sailing sytems": hydraulic or electrical winches and halyards or other mechanical systems that will assist in sailing a yacht. However, the highest speeds on the water have been recorded by windsurfers, and this sector of sailing demands a unique set of rules.

2 The number, sex and nature of the crew sailing a yacht allows multiple records for a similar discipline or route. Fully crewed, single-handed and 'single-handed by a disabled sailor' records exist for circumnavigation speed attempts and this is reproduced in passage records (between two locations) and inshore sailing.

3 Seventy per cent of the Earth's surface is covered by water supplying a limitless range of locations for sailing record attempts. The WSSRC's guidelines for a speed record state that any attempt should be between "fixed points of land, fixed navigational beacons or other charted objects fixed to the land or seabed". Exceptions are made for 'straight-line', windsurfing speed records held over a 500-metre course or over one nautical mile (1,852 metres) and offshore, mid-ocean, 24-hour run records, which are recorded by GPS.

previous page *In 1909, the pioneering aviator, Louis Blériot, flew across the Channel in 37 minutes: Alain Thébault and crew set out to beat this record in February 2005 on the radical hydrofoil,* L'Hydroptère. *Averaging 33.3 knots, the team took three minutes off Blériot's time between Dover and Calais.*

below *In 2005, yachtswoman, Hilary Lister, became the first quadriplegic sailor to cross the English Channel single-handed. Using the 'sip and puff' method, Lister helmed her 26ft Soling,* Malin, *by blowing onto an instrument panel through a rubber hose, crossing from Dover to Calais in 6 hours and 13 minutes. Although the boat had been specially adapted for Lister, she experienced such discomfort that a supply of painkillers was attached to her right shoulder within reach of her lips.*

above *Described as a "classy creation" by her skipper, Bruno Peyron, catamaran* Orange II *broke the Jules Verne Trophy record for a fully crewed circumnavigation in 2005 when she sailed round the world in 50 days 16 hours 20 minutes 4 seconds.*

From A to B and beyond

A few examples of the less well-known sailing records illustrate the range responsibility held by the WSSRC:

Oldest single-handed transatlantic crossing:
Stefan Szwarnowski (GBR) aged 77 years on *Tawny Pipit* in 1989. 72 days

Longest series of non-stop circumnavigations:
Jon Saunders (AUS) on *Perry Endeavour* in 1986–88. Three circumnavigations, 1 westabout, 2 eastabout. 657 days

Fastest sailing speed over one nautical mile:
Bjorn Dunkerbek on a windsurfer in 2004. 34.44 knots

First disabled, single-handed circumnavigation:
Vincent Lauwers (AUS) on *Vision Quest* in 2000. 233 days

The Gold Race (New York – San Francisco, via Cape Horn):
Yves Parlier (FRA) and crew on *Aquitaine Innovations* in 1998. 57 days

Melbourne – Osaka (two-handed):
Grant Wharington and Scot Gilbert (AUS) on *Wild Thing* in 1995. 26 days

Montego Bay, Jamaica – Lizard Point, Cornwall:
Tony Bullimore (GBR) and Fedor Konyukhov (RUS) with nine crew, on *Scarlet Sails* in 2003. 16 days

The Jules Verne Trophy

The Jules Verne Trophy is named after the French writer and author of *Around The World In 80 Days*: a story charting the circumnavigation adventures of the fictional character, Phileas Fogg. The event is open to any size of yacht, has no limitation on crew numbers and involves sailing non-stop, around the planet, starting and finishing on a line stretching between Lizard Point and the French island of Ushant at the western entrance to the English Channel. To date, the Jules Verne has been attempted by huge multihulls capable of maintaining high speeds for extended periods.

opposite *Gale force winds lashed catamaran, ENZA, in the final miles of her Jules Verne Trophy circumnavigation. Sir Robin Knox-Johnston, Sir Peter Blake and crew sailed around the world in just under 75 days.*

below *American aviator, balloonist and serial record breaker, Steve Fossett and his crew, smashed the transatlantic sailing record on 125ft (38.1m)* Cheyenne *in 2001.*

Jules Verne Trophy holders:

1993–94
Bruno Peyron (FRA)
Explorer (catamaran)
79 days

1994–95
Robin Knox-Johnston (GBR) and Peter Blake (NZ)
Enza (catamaran)
74 days

1997
Olivier de Kersauson (FRA)
Sport Elec (trimaran)
71 days

2002
Bruno Peyron
Orange (catamaran)
64 days

2004*
Olivier de Kersauson
Geronimo (trimaran)
63 days

2005
Bruno Peyron
Orange II (catamaran)
50 days

*Round-the-world racing was hit by controversy in 2004–05 when American yachtsman, Steve Fosset, sailed the route of the Jules Verne in 58 days on *Cheyenne*. Fosset chose not to pay the 30,000 euros entry fee required for a Jules Verne Trophy challenge and his record attempt was not recognized, although the WSSRC ratified his circumnavigation as a world record.

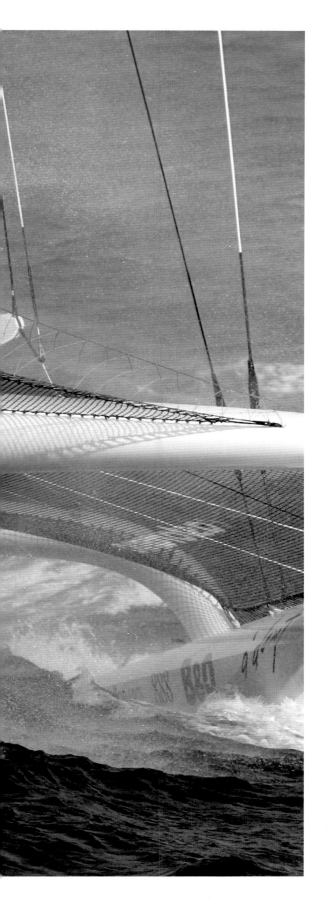

The fastest women on the planet

On 7 February 2005, British yachtswoman, Ellen MacArthur, sailed her 22.9-metre trimaran, *B&Q*, across the finish line between Lizard and Ushant completing a non-stop, solo circumnavigation in 71 days 14 hours 18 minutes 33 seconds to become the fastest person to sail alone around the world. MacArthur's entire voyage was paced against the previous record holder, Francis Joyon, who had set an exceptional time on a larger and far older trimaran, *IDEC*. When the legendary French yachtsman smashed the existing solo circumnavigation time by 21 days, many considered that the record would remain unbreakable for years to come.

The achievements of both Joyon and MacArthur are outstanding, but the two attempts were approached with very different methods. Joyon's record attempt was undertaken with a minimal budget on a yacht designed for fully crewed racing: a yacht that had already circumnavigated the world as Olivier de Kersauson's *Sport Elec* during a Jules Verne Trophy attempt seven years earlier (Joyon also used de Kersauson's ancient mainsail). MacArthur's immaculately managed and fully funded campaign was launched with a new, state of the art trimaran bristling with technology. The methods of communication also differed widely between these two skippers. After finishing his round the world trip, Francis Joyon became agitated by clamouring media attention and the throng of journalists crowding round *IDEC* on the pontoons in France and commented wearily: "A boat is a way of seeing and experiencing the oceans, NOT a method of communication." Conversely, Ellen MacArthur is supremely skilled in engaging armchair sailors and conveying the thrills, terror and hardship of circumnavigating the globe single-handed and recording the extraordinary power and beauty of the sea.

> ## I often thought about Ellen when she was in some difficult patches with winds and squalls violently pouring down on the boat

Francis Joyon, shortly after Ellen MacArthur beat his solo circumnavigation record

A selection of Ellen MacArthur's comments from her record breaking solo circumnavigation:

previous page *In 2005, Ellen MacArthur and trimaran,* B&Q, *set a new, single-handed sailing world record by circumnavigating the globe in 71 days: MacArthur beat the existing record of French yachtsman, Francis Joyon, by just 32 hours.*

"Everything is flying around the cabin - I have to hold on to something the whole time to stop being flung across the boat... I've had my head smashed against the hull a few times by the violent motion."
Encountering 30-knot winds in the South Atlantic after 15 days at sea

"It's like sailing over mountains... it's like driving an all-terrain vehicle very fast over mountains."
At 43° South, shortly after rounding the Cape of Good Hope and entering the Indian Ocean

"The beauty of those immense, rolling waves is endless and there is a kind of eternal feeling about their majestic rolling that will live on forever."

Heading further south after 23 days at sea

"To be surfing at 25-28 knots in that amount of breeze in those waves, to be handling as well as she did - I was just absolutely over the moon with her performance... it was fantastic."
Passing north of the Crozet Islands 20 hours ahead of Joyon's record

"I've been stressed all night - so stressed. I've got a cracking headache, hardly had any sleep and I've been so stressed my tongue's come out in ulcers."
Christmas Day in 35–45 knots

"There are birds around me - that's always a sign of an iceberg. There's thick fog; I can't see more than a few boat lengths in front of me. This is pretty scary..."
New Year's Eve after 34 days alone at sea, 670 miles south-west of New Zealand

"I dragged myself off the floor where I was huddled in my oilskins under a fleece blanket and looked to the sky to see yet another demon black cloud."
After 40 days at sea, preparing for a monstrous storm west of Cape Horn

"It is going to hit us. We can't get away from this one..."

Christmas Eve in the Southern Ocean as a massive low-pressure system hurtles towards the trimaran

"We're still 10,000 miles from home. We're in a boat that's getting tired, a skipper that's getting tired – mentally and emotionally zonked."
Approaching a dangerous level of fatigue after foul weather in the Southern Ocean

"I've put everything in – my heart, my soul, my flesh, my blood, just everything. I've never pushed this hard."

MacArthur slips 10 hours behind Joyon's record as wind speeds drop to below 4 knots in the South Atlantic

"Main halyard is creaking, everything is groaning, runners are stretching and there's nothing I can do. I've tried slowing down, I've tried speeding up... I've tried everything, but the fact is we've got mountains heading towards us. This God-damned low that's been sat on our nose."
Headwinds slow progress on day 49 north-east of the Falkland Islands in the South Atlantic

"I feel like I've been beaten up this morning... stiff as hell and moving around with the speed and elegance of an arthritic robot."
Having completed two mast climbs to repair damage after 22,000 miles of sailing

"We're getting a bit closer everyday, bit by bit. As long as the wind keeps blowing we'll make it home one way or the other... as long as we don't do anything stupid."
Passing the Cape Verde Islands in the North Atlantic and pulling back a two-day lead over Francis Joyon's record

"We had a few really big waves in the night – I was virtually thrown out of the bunk by one that broke right over the boat filled the cockpit... It was good I had the door shut."

The final night at sea approaching the finishing line of Ushant. Ellen MacArthur beats Francis Joyon's record by 1 day and 8 hours.

"I cannot articulate how I feel, I doubt I shall ever be able to express what this trip has put me through, or continues to put me through."
On the 69th day at sea, light winds west of Spain hinder progress and threaten the record attempt as B&Q nears the finish line

"Going to be lucky to come through this without breaking something or capsizing, to be frank, because it's already really rough and it's going to get really, really rough. The waves are going to be absolutely huge and we're going to be going straight across them which is the worst thing you could possibly do. I'm really worried."
Rounds Cape Finisterre heading into the Bay of Biscay with the prospect of Force 8–9 winds

9

Extreme Cruising

- SWINGING THE LANTERN

- THE DOS AND DON'TS
  OF CRUISING

- THE BROTHERHOOD
  OF THE COAST

- THE WAY THEY WERE

Swinging the lantern

Offer to show a friend or colleague photographs of a recent cruising holiday and the reaction can be short-term indulgence or a brief period of tolerance. Like wedding pictures, snaps of a cruising holiday can be formulaic: the crew drinking cocktails in the cockpit, children playing in the yacht's dinghy, golden sand fringing a clear-water lagoon, the boat heeling over under sail with the owner helming, etc. It is very difficult to convey the thrill of cruising on a yacht through photographs alone. How can a picture transmit the sense of adventure and freedom gained when sailing a yacht, the feeling of independence and mobility or the friendships made while at sea or in port? For this reason, cruising's verbal tradition and the ability to discuss sailing and boats in extraordinary detail for prolonged periods is an integral component of the sport: a skill known as "swinging the lantern".

All successful yachtsmen – both racing and cruising – must be proficient in the telling of yarns: a talent that can be studied and learnt in pubs, bars and yacht clubs at every sailing destination on the planet. The ability to entertain fellow yachtsmen or impressionable cruising novices with sailing tales is vital, but a sailor should also be confident in contributing to any conversation on navigation, boat handling, yacht maintenance, local customs and the global price of spare or replacement parts. Wander along a marina pontoon anywhere in the world and the sound of cruising yachtsmen swapping stories accompanies the 'clink' of loose halyards slapping against aluminium masts.

previous page *Eric Tabarly's yacht,* Côte d'Or, *in 1987 sailing past two 'pinnacle' bergs 10 miles south of Newfoundland.*

above *Modern history's most committed cruising yachtsman, St Brendan of Ardfert. The Irish monk and his crew sailed around the North Atlantic during the 6th century searching for the 'Land of Delight'. Unlike St Brendan, modern yachtsmen are unlikely to encounter man-eating fish, gryphons, fire breathing dragons, raving hermits, talking birds and "various monsters of the deep".*

opposite top *The Lemaire Channel between Booth Island and the mainland Antarctic Peninsular is aptly named 'Kodak Valley'.*

opposite bottom *Steel-hulled yacht* Seal *has a close encounter with an iceberg in Greenland's Nuuk fjord system. A majority of the North Atlantic's bergs originate from 100 glaciers along the country's western coast.*

Heaven protects children, sailors and drunken men

Mid-19th century proverb

The do's and don'ts of cruising

For the novice sailor, stepping into the alien environment of a cruising yacht can be a tense experience. The observant beginner will quickly appreciate that going sailing involves a range of equipment that is not normally encountered on dry land. It soon becomes apparent, also, that sliding gracefully through crystal clear waters demands considerable co-ordination, a comprehensive knowledge of the sea and a degree of advanced planning: an understanding of these features will enhance the enjoyment of cruising. Every cruising yacht operates under a different regime, but in most cases the skipper wields supreme authority on board: a sailing yacht is not a true democracy. If the owner or skipper is of the variety who enjoys humorous plaques, a small sign screwed in a visible position on the boat declaring that "The Skipper is Always Right" (or similar) will inform all crew as to the nature of command on the forthcoming cruise.

On many boats the crew will be given a briefing before departure and this may often answer important questions or concerns for the novice cruiser. It is impossible to investigate all aspects of sailing or cruising in an informal, pre-sail chat, but the basics on safety, the route, a destination (if any) and the weather that is likely to be encountered are significant factors. Further information can be acquired by talking with experienced members of the crew without distracting the yacht's skipper who will usually be absorbed in running the boat. Very large books have been filled with advice and instructions on cruising, but a few fundamental guidelines can prove invaluable for the beginner on his first outing:

Boarding a yacht:

Footwear is crucial in making a favourable first impression. **Don't** wear hard-bottomed shoes or black soles as both can leave easily traceable tracks on teak or fibreglass decks. **Do** check the soles of your shoes for chewing gum and other street grime. On many boats, a basket or box will be located on deck: this is not evidence of a ship's cat, but indicates that shoes should be removed.

If the boat is 'rafted' in a marina and it becomes necessary to cross another yacht to reach your cruiser, it is customary to walk around the front of the intervening boat's mast, never through the cockpit. **Don't** stumble through a yacht's cockpit uninvited as this breaches cruising etiquette and infringes unwritten territorial rules.

Once on board, **don't** throw your luggage on to the largest, most comfortable bed. This 'bunk' or 'berth' is likely to be reserved for the skipper or owner and such presumption will cause acrimony. It is often best to place your bag in a visible position that does not obstruct crew movement and hope that a berth will soon be allocated. In addition, **don't** begin unpacking your belongings immediately: space is at a premium on board and observing experienced crew activity is essential to learn the art of stowing gear.

"There is a type of yachtsman whose boat is so full of things – mostly junk – that there is scarcely room to move about. Such a boat will be congested with such objects as old condemned ropes, leaky oil cans, discarded portions of Primus stove, empty boxes, picture postcards, broken shackles, paint tins with small deposits of hardened paint on the bottom…"

Patrick Boyle, from *Sailing in a Nutshell*, published 1938

above *Queuing for fuel, queuing for supplies at the supermarket, endless paperwork issues with foreign port authorities and complex currency conversion calculations are absent on a cruise around Greenland.*

At sea:

Do pay special attention to the boom (the horizontal spar attached to the rear side of the mast at the bottom of the mainsail). Depending on the helming and communication skills of the skipper, this object can sweep across the boat without warning and deliver a blow to the head that may prove fatal. When sailing, **don't** sit on any static ropes or pieces of deck gear: a boat requires constant attention and ropes and equipment are liable to suddenly move at alarming speeds. This can result in unpleasant rope burns to the buttocks or the loss of fingers.

When sailing, **don't** sit on the companionway. On smaller and medium sized yachts this ladder is often the busiest access point between the deck and interior of a boat. Although it is one of the most comfortable places to sit on any boat, you will be an obstruction to any crew movement and test the patience of those on board. It is valuable to remember the sailing adage: "Only admirals and ****holes sit on the companionway".

For many beginners, a yacht's plumbing can cause more fear than the prospect of storms and mountainous seas. **Don't** risk using the onboard lavatory (or 'heads' as they are often known) without instruction from an expert in this field. Marine plumbing on smaller boats is unreliable and has a notoriously high failure rate. Any embarrassment that may be felt through repeatedly asking for clear and precise instructions on the use of the heads is preferable to the drama and shame caused by improper or over enthusiastic use of the equipment.

Don't enter into an argument if the skipper shouts at you. He may be concerned for your safety or the safety of the yacht and yelling a command or warning may be the most effective method of communicating his concern. It is unwise to bear a grudge when you may be forced to spend the next six hours, six days or six weeks in close confinement. Once you are ashore, it is an **essential** sailing tradition that you buy the skipper drinks however abusive or unpleasant he has been while you were at sea.

The Brotherhood of the Coast

There are hundreds of yacht cruising clubs and associations scattered around the globe, but none are as curious as The Brotherhood of the Coast (Hermandad de la Costa, Les Frères de la Côte, Brüder der Küste etc.): an international cruising fellowship founded by yachtsmen in Santiago, Chile during the early 1950s. From Angola, West Africa, to Orange Beach, Alabama, this fraternity of sailors exists to share the pleasures of cruising between like-minded yachtsmen.

When visiting yacht clubs in distant and hard-to-reach areas of the world it is often possible to spot a trophy left by visiting members of The Brotherhood nestling among the dusty collection of souvenirs in the club's bar. Should you wonder at the origin of the obscure flag showing an anchor with twin stars and crossed oars on a black background (reminiscent of the Jolly Roger flag of piracy), it is evidence that The Brotherhood has reached this yachting outpost before you. The author can confirm that the mysterious Brotherhood has left its mark in the world's southernmost yacht club, the Micalvi Club de Yates just 80 miles north of Cape Horn. Indeed, intrepid sailors from the Valparaiso chapter of the society have even left an inscription a few metres from the infamous cape's lighthouse.

Although The Brotherhood are quick to distance themselves from any association with quasi-secret societies or politically motivated groups, their hierarchy system reveals a familiar fondness for arcane orders of rank shared by Masonic organisations. A senior figure in The Brotherhood – 'Big Brother' – is supported by the 'Grand Scribe' and assisted by the 'Guard of The Treasury', who wields power over 'The Keeper of The Powder Keg'. Whether any members hold enough authority to order the execution of junior Brothers is unclear. Any yachtsmen who may fear encountering The Brotherhood on the high seas should be aware that all members must adhere to the fraternity's unbreakable Eight Commandments. The first commandment in this cruising credo demands that a Brother must "Obey with respect [his] Captain's orders". If this limit to lawlessness fails to inspire confidence, Commandment Five instructs acolytes: "Do not be envious of your brother's ship nor his sails or motors". The final Commandment confirms that The Brotherhood are a peaceful and benign group of yachtsmen who should not be feared or avoided and advises that "The love of the ocean should be the following cult of your days".

left: *Nerves of steel and precise crew co-ordination are required to negotiate the Antarctic Peninsular. Any damage sustained by a yacht cruising in remote areas must be rectified by the crew.*

The way we were

When yacht cruising experienced a renaissance in the 1950s after a period of post World War II austerity, it was necessary that newcomers to the sport received expert guidance. One of England's most experienced and eloquent sailors, Peter Heaton, achieved great success in this field and published the invaluable book, *Cruising*, in 1953. Although the language, style and presentation have changed since Heaton's era, reproducing some examples of his expert advice shows that little has changed in over half a century:

A warning to potential cruisers:

If you are accustomed to going to sea after lunch and returning in time for dinner, you will find that it may take a bit of time getting used to the more complicated routine of cruising.

The joy of navigation:

The ability to navigate a yacht far out of sight of land and to pilot her to the harbour of his choice increases man's self respect, his usefulness to his country in times of stress, and, perhaps most important of all, his own pleasure.

A different breed:

No one who has sailed a small yacht during a passage lasting more than 24 hours, taking day and night and weather in his stride, can fail to feel a sense of achievement and that feeling of participation in the freemasonry of the sea that sets seamen apart from the ordinary chap.

Essentials:

Unlike the racing sailor, who doesn't mind getting wet through, the cruising man, if he is to enjoy his cruise, must keep his inner garments dry.

Offshore dangers:

Beware of zip-fasteners at sea; they rapidly become utterly demoralized by the salt atmosphere, and refuse to function.

Motorized power:

There are many people who feel quite strongly about this 'mechanical topsail' business. There exists a kind of snobbery about it all – 'one just doesn't have an engine!' Be that as it may there are times when an engine can be very useful.

above *Yacht* Pelagic *in front of a 'drydock' iceberg in Fournier Bay on the Antarctic Peninsular. Icebergs are categorized in to five further types: tabular (medium freeboard, smooth topped), non-tabular (medium freeboard, irregular surface), blocky (sheer, tall sides), pinnacle (pyramid or mountain shaped) and wedge.*

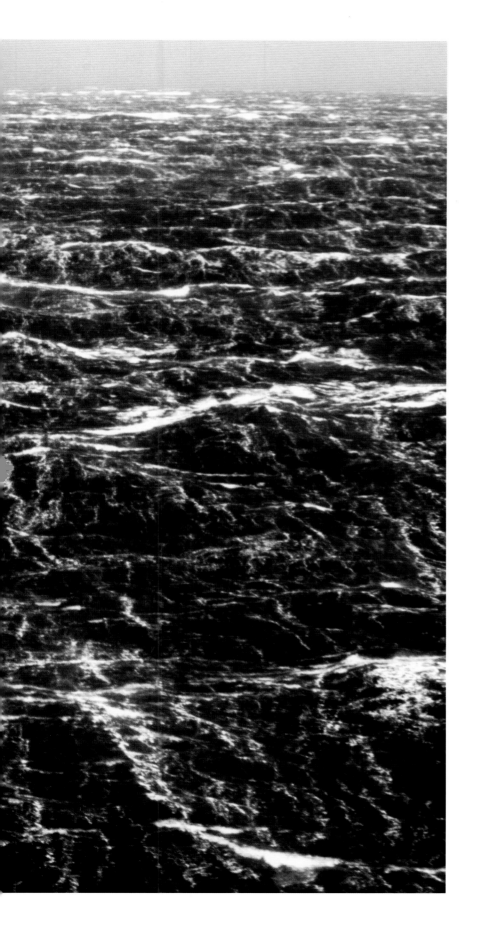

10

The Southern Ocean

- A TOURIST GUIDE

- SURVIVAL TIPS

- MAYDAY! MAYDAY! MAYDAY!

- CAPE HORN AND
  THE ALBATROSS

A tourist guide

Early in 2000, the International Hydrographic Organisation ratified the existence of a fifth ocean to join the watery realms of the Atlantic, Arctic, Pacific and Indian Oceans. Technically, the Southern Ocean comprises the sea area extending north from the coast of Antarctica to Latitude 60° South. For deep-water sailors, though, passing through the Roaring Forties (Latitude 40° South) into the Furious Fifties (Latitude 50° South) signifies entering this hostile environment. Those sailing further south, below the limit of the Antarctic Convergence – a defined, mid-ocean border where water temperatures differ by margins of 2–3°C north-south – and into the Screaming Sixties, penetrate the most remote ocean zone on the planet.

The Southern Ocean covers an area just over twice the size of North America with maximum depths ranging between 4,000–5,000 metres. The strongest average wind strengths on Earth blast across this area from the west, building tremendous seas from an eastward flowing current that rolls around the planet unchecked by any landmass until the treacherous funnel between South America and Antarctica at Cape Horn. In a region that is furthest from the reach of any rescue services, yachtsmen encounter gales, monstrous waves, persistent boat-breaking conditions and the threat of icebergs: the Southern Ocean is no place for the faint at heart.

previous page *The Southern Ocean contains the highest average wave sizes on Earth. 60-80 knot winds (Hurricane Force 12) and 12-15 metre waves are captured on film from the upper deck of a French training warship,* Jeanne d'Arc, *en-route to Cape Horn.*

below *A lone albatross patrols the Southern Ocean off the Sub-Antarctic island of South Georgia, 2,000 km east of Cape Horn at 54° South. Superstitious yachtsmen claim that each albatross carries the soul of a drowned sailor.*

opposite *Jean Pierre Dick and* Virbac *experienced one of the roughest Horn roundings during the 2004-05 Vendée Globe. Shortly after passing the world's southernmost cape, the French skipper made a brief satellite call to the race office: "It's extraordinary! I rounded with 45 knots established winds with 55 knots at times. It was raining and conditions were a little extreme. What satisfaction. It's a childhood dream come true."*

Survival tips

Shortly before the start of the 2004–05 Vendée Globe, single-handed, non-stop, round the world race, British skipper Mike Golding described sailing conditions in the Southern Ocean: "The South is just one long chain of being afraid, to being happy, to having just survived." A very experienced high latitude sailor, Golding knew the conditions he would have to endure for thirty days: "You're in a reefed down sail plan, the boat is barrelling along at top speed, she's on the boil… you just monitor it." During the race, French skipper Jean Le Cam on *Bonduelle* explained the dilemma facing skippers attempting to preserve their boats while continuing to sail at a competitive pace: "If you hoist too much sail you zoom off like a locomotive and risk slamming into waves and seeing your mast collapse. It's like walking a tightrope."

Does the sun exist? I haven't seen it for quite a while.

Patrice Carpentier enters the Southern Ocean on *VM Matériaux* during the 2004–05 Vendée Globe

left, top *A snow blizzard hits the Global Challenge fleet in the high latitudes of the Southern Ocean. Gale force winds, monstrous waves, thick fog and the threat of icebergs sustain the fearsome reputation of this remote area.*

left, bottom *Surfing Southern Ocean waves demands helming skill, nerves of steel and intense concentration from the helmsman of a Global Challenge yacht. On the early clipper ships, helmsmen were forbidden from looking over their shoulder in case the towering waves bearing down from astern should cause a distraction and endanger the boat.*

To combat the brutal physical conditions encountered sailing through the Southern Ocean, skippers endeavour to maintain a sleep routine and increase their calorie intake to counteract the effects of freezing conditions – a difficult and dull task when food is limited to a repetitive series of freeze-dried or irradiated (pre-cooked) meals. Safeguarding the boat and reducing the chances of sustaining personal injury or – in the worst case – being washed overboard, is paramount and the resulting mental stress can be acute. In the 2004–05 Vendée Globe, British yachtsman, Conrad Humphreys, pushed himself and his Open 60, *Hellomoto*, to the very limit of endurance. Humphreys overhauled eight of his competitors during a month in the Southern Ocean between the Cape of Good Hope and Cape Horn, but this extraordinary achievement extracted a heavy toll: "My body did not sense the extreme fatigue and shutdown. It allowed me to drift into a stage beyond exhaustion, where my world suddenly seemed to contain only obstacles and no solutions. For someone that does not see obstacles in life, this world was immeasurably depressing."

below *Vendée Globe skipper, Conrad Humphreys, checks his route to the finish line as he sails* Hellomoto *round Cape Horn in January 2005 after 74 days alone at sea. The British skipper was rewarded with a benign rounding after overhauling eight competing yachts between the Cape of Good Hope and Cape Horn during 40 days and 10,500 miles of tough Southern Ocean racing.*

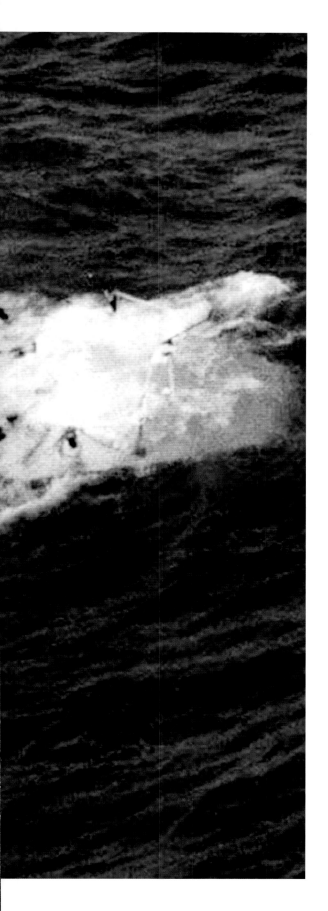

Mayday! Mayday! Mayday!

In 1996, yachtsman Raphaël Dinelli took part in the third edition of the Vendée Globe race as an unofficial entry. Dinelli's preparation for the race had overrun, leaving him unable to complete a qualifying ocean passage and enter the race officially; but this setback was not going to stop the French yachtsman fulfilling his dream of circumnavigating the world. The Southern Ocean, however, turned this dream into the blackest nightmare.

In 65-knot winds reaching gusts of 80 knots, Dinelli's yacht, *Algimouss*, capsized and refused to right herself. The mast soon shattered and – still connected to the rigging – began smashing holes into the upturned yacht as the boat was thrown around by violent wave action. Freezing water poured into the boat and mixed with diesel leaking from the fuel tanks. Vomiting from the effects of fumes, Dinelli was able to locate and activate the yacht's distress beacon. Finally, the violent motion of the sea wore through the rigging, the mast detached and *Algimouss* rolled upright. Battered by 50ft seas, Dinelli launched the liferaft, attaching it to his stricken yacht with a short line. This done, he strapped himself into the swamped cockpit and took stock of the situation. With all the electronic equipment on board flooded and useless, Dinelli had no way of knowing whether his distress signal had been successfully transmitted or received by the race organisation or rescue services. As *Algimouss* settled lower in the water as successive waves smashed across her semi-submerged decks, the yachtsman prepared for the longest and, possibly, the last night of his life. Then, shortly before nightfall as Dinelli spoke to his yacht encouraging and willing her to stay afloat, the line attaching his liferaft parted and the bright orange inflatable sanctuary tumbled across the waves, disappearing downwind....

Subjected to similar conditions experienced by Dinelli, British Vendée Globe skipper Pete Goss was close to exhaustion on 50ft *Aqua Quorum*, 160 miles downwind from *Algimouss*. A flashing light on the

141

left *Stranded 1,200 miles south west of Australia, Raphaël Dinelli stands on* Algimouss *as she sinks deeper into the abyss of the Southern Ocean during the 1996–97 Vendée Globe. Dinelli's liferaft had been lost overnight and a spare was dropped by the Royal Australian Air Force just minutes before the yacht sank entirely.*

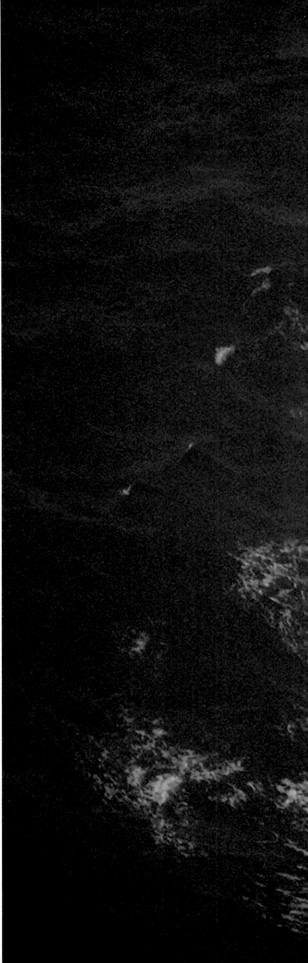

satellite communications display mounted above the chart table alerted Goss of an incoming message from the race organisation and he quickly read through the details of Dinelli's catastrophe. It was clear that *Aqua Quorum* was the only yacht in the area and Dinelli's survival depended entirely upon Goss. Reaching Dinelli meant turning the boat around and heading directly into gale-force winds and mountainous seas, but the ex-Royal Marine commando was pragmatic about this monumental task and later commented: "It was simple; the decision had been made for me a long time ago by a tradition of the sea. When someone is in trouble, you help".

At daylight, a plane from the Royal Australian Air Force (RAAF) flew low over *Algimouss* and dropped a liferaft. Grabbing some supplies, Dinelli scrambled inside and found a written message telling him that Pete Goss was 10 hours away. Just five minutes after boarding the liferaft, the French yachtsman watched his boat sink to the bottom of the Southern Ocean. Meanwhile, *Aqua Quorum* was beating to windward, constantly knocked flat by winds, burying her spreaders in the sea every half an hour. With frequent updates from the race organisation in France and the Marine Rescue Control Centre (MRCC) in Australia, Goss carefully monitored his progress towards the position of Dinelli and his yacht. After one such check, it became clear that Goss had overshot and he turned the yacht around, dropped the mainsail and sailed under a storm jib, constantly zigzagging downwind at 3–4 knots searching for Dinelli in the huge waves, firing flares and sounding his fog horn. With impeccable timing the RAAF reappeared, dropping smoke canisters and flashing the aircraft's landing lights, guiding Goss through mountainous seas towards the liferaft. Having made visual contact with Dinelli, Goss threw two fenders attached to a line over the stern as an extra precaution should he fail to grab him on his first pass, and then released the jib halyard and cautiously approached.

Dinelli's extraordinary will to survive on a sinking yacht and his rescue by a fellow sailor ignited the public's interest in single-handed sailing and the story of endurance and courage is a fundamental cornerstone of solo sailing folklore. Goss delivered Dinelli to Hobart, Tasmania, before continuing the circumnavigation and later received the Legion d'Honneur from President Chirac of France for his outstanding bravery. Eight years after losing his yacht in the Southern Ocean – an experience that would deter many from re-entering the area afloat – Dinelli successfully completed the 2004–05 Vendée Globe.

142

right *British skipper Pete Goss turned his yacht around, then sailed 160 miles to windward through the Southern Ocean in hurricane conditions and rescued Dinelli. Later, in an Inmarsat message to his wife, Goss wrote: "I had a good Christmas because I saved a man's life and he is OK. I'm sailing home as fast as I can" (from* Close To The Wind *by Pete Goss).*

Cape Horn and the Albatross

Since its discovery in 1616, Cape Horn has been a craved destination and rite of passage for offshore sailors: a prime objective in sailing aspirations, part maritime bogeyman, part Holy Grail. The Horn marks the northern limit of Drake Passage, a fearsome stretch of water between South America and the Antarctic continent where the Southern Ocean is squeezed through a narrow and relatively shallow gap: a concentration of wind and waves that can produce monstrous seas. The cape's legendary status and fearsome reputation has filled the pages of many books, but the "*Long Drag Shanty*" conveys a true sense of dread that the area can inspire:

> *Round Cape Horn where the stiff wind blows,*
> *Round Cape Horn where there's sleet and snow.*
> *I wish to God I'd never been born*
> *To drag my carcass around Cape Horn*

Cape Horn has wrecked countless ships and claimed the lives of many sailors attempting to round this barren, rocky outcrop – the southernmost drowned peak of the Andes mountain chain. One survivor of a Horn gale was Charles Darwin during the voyage of exploration that formed his theories on evolution. This experience totally demoralized the brilliant naturalist: "The necessary discomforts of the ship heavily pitching and the miseries of constant wet and cold, I have scarcely for an hour been quite free from seasickness. How long the bad weather may last, I know not; but my spirits, temper, and stomach, I am well assured, will not hold out much longer."

Darwin's ship, the *Beagle*, came within minutes of foundering during the gale due to the captain's insistence that all the ports for deck drains should remain closed. Fortunately, the ship's carpenter chose to remain on standby with a handspike and saved the *Beagle*. Darwin's diary entry of Sunday 13 January, 1833 records this event, just 20 miles west of the cape:

> "*Our horizon was limited to a small compass by the spray carried by the wind; the sea looked ominous; there was so much foam, that it resembled a dreary plain covered by patches of drifted snow. At noon the storm was at its height; and we began to suffer; a great sea struck us and came onboard; the same sea filled our decks so deep, that if another had followed it is not difficult to guess the result. It is not easy to imagine what a state of confusion the decks were in from the great body of water. At last the ports were knocked open and she again rose buoyant to the sea.*"

Although Darwin was clearly in a poor condition during the storm, he was still able make observations: "Whilst we were heavily labouring, it was curious to see how the albatross with its widely expanded wings, glided right up the wind". These solitary creatures symbolize the Southern Ocean. Their ability to harness the fierce winds raging at the bottom of the world coupled with a habit of following yachts and ships through remote sea areas has formed a mysterious bond between sailors and albatross: a connection that is highly evident at Cape Horn. There are only five manmade structures on treeless Horn Island. At the southern tip of the island sits an unmanned lighthouse marking Cape Horn and a second light is located above Point Espocon on the eastern end of the island. Behind the second light is a single-storey, 20m x 15m, six-room hut housing the Chilean lighthouse keeper and his family. Alongside the dwelling is a tiny chapel: a simple building constructed in timber, housing six pews and a plain, unfussy altar. Upon closing this building's double doors on the gale outside, the quiet within the chapel is entirely unnatural. This almost supernatural aspect increases with the final structure; a massive albatross statue dominating the plain above the island's southern cliffs. This diamond-shaped iron artwork features a cutout silhouette of an albatross in flight: aligned north-south, the prevailing westerly wind moans through the statue's void, producing a primal and highly disturbing sound. Carved on the concrete base of the statue is a sombre and melancholy poem in Spanish. It is very difficult **145** to turn one's back on the giant albatross:

> *I am the Albatross Waiting for You*
> *At the End of the World*
> *I am the Forgotten Soul of Dead Sailors*
> *Those who Sailed Through Cape Horn*
> *From All Oceans in the World.*
> *But they have Not Died*
> *In The Furious Waves,*
> *In My Wings they Fly today*
> *To The Eternity*
> *In The Last Crevice*
> *Of Antarctic Winds*

Sara Vial. December 1992

top *Albatross are often the only wildlife that deep ocean sailors will encounter. These magnificent birds represent the solitude and isolation of the Southern Ocean.*

left *Cape Horn's mystical status and cruel reputation becomes evident in gale force conditions. At 55° South, Horn Island is said to be the grave of 800 ships and 10,000 sailors lost at sea attempting to round the tip of South America.*

11

When It All Goes Horribly Wrong

- TRADITIONAL SAFEGUARDS

- WHAT TO PACK, WHAT TO LEAVE ONSHORE AND THE PROBLEM WITH RABBITS

- WHISTLING, WOMEN AND PRIESTS: TRICKY ISSUES

- WISE WORDS

Traditional safeguards

It is logical that a sport with so many inherent dangers should have a long and complicated tradition of taboo and superstition – a tradition that continues to flourish in our modern, secular society. Sailing superstitions differ between countries and cultures, though many are universal. Beginning a voyage on Friday is considered highly unlucky by sailors around the world, although few will realize that this stems from the Crucifixion being carried out just before the weekend. Other non-sailing days include the first Monday in April (Cain's birthday and the day on which Abel was killed), the second Monday in August (the day on which Sodom and Gomorrah were destroyed) and 31 December (the day on which Judas Iscariot hanged himself).

An auspicious launching is essential to limit any disasters befalling a new vessel. The seemingly harmless tradition of baptising a boat by smashing a bottle of champagne over her bow or – in the continental style – pouring wine over her decks, has its roots in the disturbing custom practised by Ancient Greeks of dragging a newly launched galley down a slipway covered in chained and bound slaves, washing the keel in blood from the crushed bodies. The Vikings continued this cruel theme by executing prisoners – or possibly any non-sailor loitering nearby – on a new longboat's deck. Today's innocuous ceremony is still fraught with superstition and should the champagne bottle fail to burst on the first swing, many sailors will wring their hands and crack their knuckles in agitation while muttering about cursed ships and doomed crews.

above *Heading for Padstow, Cornwall, under sail and motor in May 1995, disaster struck the 137 year-old tall ship,* Maria Assumpta. *Engine failure and a lee shore saw the boat smash into rocks and founder quickly: three crewmembers lost their lives in the wreck.*

left *Gusts of 50 knots, an open foredeck hatch, a forward compartment full of water and two waves over the bow send* Silk II *"down the mine" in Cowes Week 1996. One crewmember disappeared over the*

side and was swiftly recovered while
the bowman bravely held on as he was
plunged 4 meters underwater. The
44ft yacht sustained a few bent stanchions
and went on to win the Britannia Cup the
following day.

previous page *Worst case scenario:*
Théodore Géricault's Raft of the Medusa.
In 1816 the Medusa *left France sailing
to Senegal, West Africa. After running
aground on the Arguin Bank off Morocco,*

a raft measuring 65 x 23 ft was built
from the ship's masts and timbers:
150 passengers and crew were cast adrift
while the captain and his 'friends' set off in
the ship's boats. Fighting and gang warfare
broke out on the raft and soon the
survivors began devouring flesh from
corpses. Only 15 men were rescued
after 13 days adrift when the raft was
discovered just 4 miles off the coast. The
artist studied corpses and body parts from
a hospital for added realism.

What to pack, what to leave onshore and the problem with rabbits

above *Loïck Peyron's trimaran,* Fujifilm, *began to disintegrate in huge seas, snapping her starboard float between the crossbeams during the single-handed Route du Rhum of 2002. Determined to "bring the baby back home", Peyron sailed through 45 knot winds under bare poles: "The waves are 6–10 meters high, it's white everywhere, really beautiful. I now have to remember my boy scout years to make repairs." Unable to withstand the battering, the yacht later dismasted.*

opposite *Dismasted yacht,* Stand Aside, *tows a liferaft in the Tasman Sea during the 1998 Sydney-Hobart Race. Hurricane strength winds ripped through the 115 boats racing from Australia to Tasmania with tragic results: 66 yachts retired from racing, 5 boats sank, a total of 55 yachtsmen were rescued and 6 lives were lost.*

Before the introduction of buoyancy aids, emergency flares and the invention of the EPIRB (Emergency Position Indicating Radio Beacon), a highly prized item to prevent drowning was the caul from a newborn baby. This filmy membrane that often covers the head at birth was an essential talisman for sailors: newspaper advertisements offered large sums of money for remnants of the amniotic sac, and midwives could earn a considerable bonus.

Flowers on board are generally considered to bring bad luck and are destined to form a floating wreath as a vessel sinks into the abyss – a superstition that is still strongly held on many submarines. On Italian boats, any green-coloured clothing is forbidden and green boats in general are considered unlucky, as is carrying an umbrella, fitting a yacht with a new tiller and the eating of pears. On British boats, bananas are often discouraged. Italians realize that sailing on Friday is out of the question, but Thursday is also considered a bit of a gamble.

Many Spanish sailors will not allow books by the Argentine solo circumnavigator, Vito Dumas, to be kept or read on board. The Spanish also maintain that if a crewmember steps on deck having dressed carelessly with a shirt, jacket or trousers inside out or back-to-front, disaster will soon occur and the offending article of clothing is hastily thrown overboard, often while it is still worn by the negligent sailor. Bringing a black cat on to a boat heralds good fortune, but ensure that you step on deck right foot first.

The most rigorously obeyed superstition on French boats involves rabbits. The aversion to this animal can result in a farmhouse pâté that may contain traces of rabbit meat being tossed over the side followed by anything showing a picture of the detested creature or books on suspect, woodland topics. The mere mention of rabbits on, or near, a French boat can have dire consequences. If a crewmember becomes overpowered by an urge to discuss the despised beast, a number of pseudonyms may be used without invoking sinister phenomena: "Le gris-gris" (the grey one), "Le cousin du lièvre" (the hare's cousin) and "le mouton a cinq pattes" (the ram with five paws). This antagonism was taken to extremes in the Indian Ocean's high latitudes during a successful Jules Verne Trophy record attempt in 2002. A message was sent from the maxi-catamaran, *Orange*, stating that the only non-French crewmember on board had been dropped off on the barren Kerguelen Islands. Frantic questions flew through the ether from race control requesting further details whereupon it transpired that the hapless Australian crewmember, Nick Moloney, had committed a massive breach of protocol while the yacht sailed through iceberg infested waters. His crime was to observe that one of the bergs looked "a bit like a rabbit", causing the horrified helmsman to crash gybe the catamaran. This merited Moloney's instant marooning at latitude 50° South. The date of this draconian punishment was 1 April.

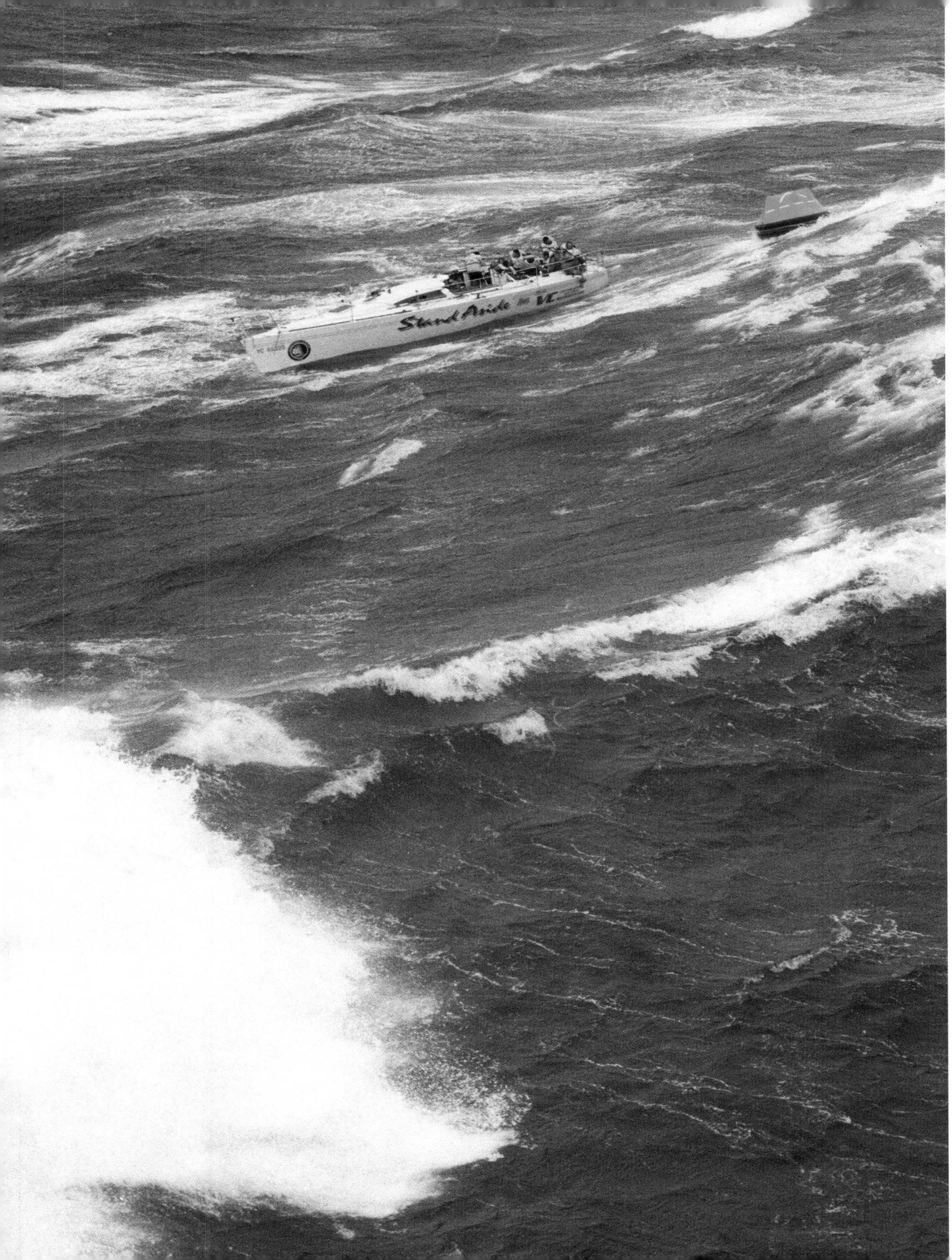
Stand Aside

left *During the 2003 Mondial Assistance race from France to Spain via the Azores Islands in the Atlantic, ORMA 60 trimaran* Foncia, *collided with a mystery object. Her steering quickly became unmanageable and the multihull was flipped upside down. While most of the crew, including Ellen MacArthur, scrambled below as the yacht inverted, skipper Alain Gautier remained on deck and became temporarily trapped in the water under the yacht's trampoline netting. Two days later, the boat arrived in Lisbon under tow.*

Whistling, women and priests: tricky issues

A woman and a ship ever want mending

Late 16th century, originally from 2nd century BC Latin

The trick with whistling at sea is knowing when to stop. It is widely agreed that whistling in calm weather can summon wind, while many sailors believe that whistling and simultaneously scratching the mast can guarantee the arrival of fresh breeze. However, whistling cheerfully in winds that are already blowing hard can court calamity and summon hurricane-force conditions. The ancient French warning to the "gabier", sitting as look-out in the crow's nest of a square rigged ship wisely advises: "Siffle, gabier, siffle pour appeler le vent, mais aussitôt le vent venu, gabier ne siffle plus" (Whistle, gabier, whistle to call the wind, but when it arrives, whistle no more).

There is an ancient belief that the sight of a woman angers the sea and men in many fishing communities would often refuse to leave shore should they meet a barefooted woman on the way to their boat. This superstition provided a convenient excuse for sailors to remain ashore in bad conditions, although – equally conveniently – should a naked woman appear before them during a storm, the immediate effect would be a calming of the wind. This tradition is the root cause of bare-breasted figureheads.

Priests are usually considered as bad omens and must be avoided immediately before setting sail. Should a mariner encounter a priest while walking to the quay before boarding a boat, it is prudent to cancel the voyage altogether. Furthermore, if the priest has red hair or is cross-eyed, a wise sailor will avoid boats for a considerable period. However, occasionally the clergy are extremely useful – especially when choosing to rename a boat. Normally, re-christening a vessel brings bad luck, but in France a system has evolved to limit this danger. On 15 August it is possible to carry out a name change if the correct rituals are adhered to. This ceremony involves sailing upwind performing a series of short tacks making a zigzag pattern, before turning the boat around and sailing downwind over the upwind route: an operation that signifies a snake eating its tail. Finally, arrange for a priest to bless the boat, but under no circumstances should he be allowed to step on board.

153

above *An Ultra 30 at the Cardiff Grand Prix in 1994. These light, super fast boats were considered the ultimate gung-ho weapon afloat... until they fell over. Requiring lightning reactions and supreme crew co-ordination, keeping an Ultra 30 upright was a constant challenge.*

Wise words

Some international examples of man's relationship with the sea:

Weather lore...

Mackerel skies and mares' tails,
Make tall ships carry short sails

If woolly fleeces deck the heavenly way
Be sure no rain will mar a summer's day

When the sea-hog (porpoise) jumps,
Stand by your pumps

First rise after low (pressure)
Foretells a stronger blow

Seagull, seagull, sit on the sand,
It's never good weather when you're on the land

When the wind shifts against the sun,
Trust it not, for back it will run.
When the wind follows the sun,
*Fine weather will never be done**
[*This holds true for northern hemisphere, but reverse the wind
 direction for southern hemisphere]

If wind is north-east three days without rain,
Eight days will pass before south again

When parrots whistle, expect rain

The wind...

The sea breeze blows the pelican where he wants to go (Corsica)

Fear blows wind into the sails (Japan)

Shipwreck and drowning...

Don't sail out farther than you can row back (Denmark)

It's too late to swim when the water is up to your lips (Denmark)

You cannot complain about the sea if you suffer shipwreck a
 second time (Iceland)

Pray to God, but continue to row for shore (Russia)

The water in which one drowns is always an ocean (Armenia)

Why jump in the water before the ship turns over? (China)

Little leaks sink big ships (England)

Captain and crew...

If you are a friend of the captain, you can wipe your hands on the sail (Arabic)

God will help a seaman in a storm, but the pilot must remain at the wheel (German)

A ship with two captains sinks (Turkey)

After a ship has sunk, everyone knows how she might have been saved (Italy)

When the sea is calm, every ship has a good captain (Sweden)

Nodding the head does not row the boat (Ireland)

What...?

If you want to drown yourself, don't torture yourself with shallow water (Bulgaria)

If the seawater were hotter, we could catch boiled fish (France)

He who sees heaven in the water, sees fish in the trees (China)

No matter how treacherous the sea, a woman will always be more so (Brittany)

The surface of the water is beautiful, but it is no good to sleep on (Ghana)

left, top *Ignoring the vital role played by running backstays had dire consequences for* Nippon *during the 1991 IACC World Championships in San Diego.*

left, bottom *In 22 knots of breeze and choppy conditions,* Team New Zealand *dismast off Auckland during the 2003 America's Cup as Swiss challenger,* Alinghi, *disappears over the horizon. The Kiwis fitted a spare mast for the final race, but the Cup was soon heading for Geneva.*

Index

Author's Acknowledgements and Sources

Further Reading:
A Narrative Of The Voyage Of HMS Beagle, edited by David Stanbury, The Folio Society
A Voyage For Madmen, Peter Nichols, Profile Books
Around The World Alone, Alain Colas, Barron's/Woodbury
Close To The Wind, Pete Goss, Headline
Cruising, Peter Heaton, Pelican Books
Gypsy Moth Circles The World, Sir Francis Chichester, World Books
In Quest Of The Sun, Alain Gerbault, Hodder and Stoughton
OSTAR: "Observer" Single-handed Transatlantic Race, GT Foulis & Co Ltd
Sailing Alone Around the World by Joshua Slocum, Penguin Classics
Sailing in a Nutshell, Patrick Boyle, Methuen & Co.
The Strange Voyage of Donald Crowhurst, Nicholas Tomalin and Ron Hall, Hodder and Stoughton
The Ultimate Challenge, Barry Pickthall, Orbis
Waters Of Wight, Douglas Phillips-Birt, Cassell
Winning In One-Designs, Dave Perry, Adlard Coles Nautical

Web sources:
www.teamellen.com
www.vendeeglobe.org
www.americascup.com
www.volvooceanrace.com
www.thedailysail.com
www.sailspeedrecords.com

Picture Acknowledgements

Anova Books Co. is committed to respecting the intellectual property rights of others. We have therefore taken all reasonable efforts to ensure that the reproduction of all content on these pages is done with the full consent of copyright owners. If you are aware of any unintentional omissions please contact the company directly so that any necessary corrections may be made for future editions.

Front Cover: Jon Nash Photography; **Back Cover:** © Jacques Vapillon; **1, 2&3** Yvan Zedda/ Bluegreen; **4** ©Ellen MacArthur/ Offshore Challenge Sailing Team; **7** ©Bettman/ CORBIS; **8** Bill Rowntree/ Knox-Johnston Archive/ PPL; **8&9** Jean-Marie Liot/ DPPI/ Offshore Challenges; **10&11** Yvan Zedda/ Bluegreen **12, 13** Photo Beken of Cowes; **14&15** Richard Langdon/ Bluegreen **16, 17** ©Jacques Vapillon; **18** Rick Tomlinson/ Bluegreen; **19** ©Jacques Vapillon; **20&21** Copyright ©1997. A. D. Blake/ Bluegreen. All Rights Reserved; **22** Photo Arnaud Février/ Bluegreen; **23**Carlo Borlenghi/ kospictures.com; **24&25** Francesco Ferri/ ACM/ SEA & See/ DPPI; **26** Christian Février/ Bluegreen; **26&27** Franck Socha/ Bluegreen; **28&29, 30** Christian Février/ Bluegreen; **32&33** Kaoru Soehata/ Bluegreen; **34,35, 36&37** Franck Socha/ Bluegreen; **39** Carlo Borlenghi/ kospictures.com; **40** Kaoru Soehata/ Bluegreen; **41** Francesco Ferri/ ACM/ SEA & See/ DPPI; **42&43, 44&45, 46, 48&49** Rick Tomlinson/ Bluegreen; **50&51** Bob Fisher/ PPL; **52** Rick Tomlinson/ Bluegreen; **53** Thomas Lundberg/ PPL; **54** Rick Tomlinson/ Bluegreen; **55** Richard Langdon/ Bluegreen; **56, 58&59** Rick Tomlinson/ Bluegreen; **61** ©Jean Guichard/ CORBIS; **62** Steven Pratt Rnas Culdrose/ Ajax News/ DPPI; **63** Gary Blake/ DPPI; **64&65** Carlo Borlenghi/ DPPI; **66,67** Daniel Forster/ DPPI; **68,70&71** marinepics.com; **72** Jacques Vapillon/ DPPI; **73T, 73B, 74&75** Carlo Borlenghi/ kospictures.com; **76&77** Bill Rowntree/ Knox-Johnston Archive/ PPL; **78** Chichester Archive/ PPL; **79** Collection Chevalier-Taglang/ DPPI; **80** Sunday Times/ Chichester Archive/ PPL; **81** Chichester Archive/ PPL; **82&83** Bill Rowntree/ Knox-Johnston Archive/ PPL; **85** PPL Archive; **86&87** ©Jacques Vapillon; **89** Chichester Archive/ PPL; **91** Photo Gilles Martin-Raget; **92&93, 94, 95** ©Jacques Vapillon; **96&97** Photo Gilles Martin-Raget; **98** Jon Nash/ DPPI; **99** Benoit Stichelbaut/ DPPI; **100B, 100&101** Yven Gladu/ DPPI; **102&103** Billy Black; **105** ©Jacques Vapillon; **106** Photo Gilles Martin-Raget; **107** ©Jacques Vapillon; **108** DPPI; **109** © Conrad Humphreys/ CHR; **110&111** Billy Black/ PPL; **112, 113** Billy Black; **114&115** Jean-Marie Liot/ DPPI; **116** ©Mark Lloyd Images; **117** Jacques Vapillon/ DPPI; **118, 119** Henri Thibault/ DPPI; **120&121** Benoit Stichelbaut/ DPPI;**124&125** Christian Février/ Bluegreen; **126** The Art Archive/ The British Library; **127T** Rick Tomlinson/ Bluegreen; **127B, 129** © Hamish Laird, 2005, www.expeditionsail.com; **130&131** Daniel Allisy/ Bluegreen; **132&133** Rick Tomlinson/ Bluegreen; **134&135** Christian Février/ Bluegreen; **136** ©Rex Features; **137** ©Jacques Vapillon; **138T** ©Kester Keighley **138B** marinepics.com; **139** © Conrad Humphreys/ CHR; **140&141** Sportshoot/ PPL; **142&143** Tony McDonough/ Sportshoot/ PPL; **144&145** ©Jacques Vapillon; **145T** Daniel Allisy/ Bluegreen; **146&147** The Art Archive/ Musée du Louvre Paris/ Dagli Orti; **148** Photo Beken of Cowes; **148&149** Nigel Bennetts/ PPL; **150** Yvan Zedda/ Bluegreen; **151** Ian Mainsbridge/ PPL; **152&153** Peter Bentley/ PPL; **152B** Yvan Zedda/ Bluegreen; **154&155T** Christian Février/ Bluegreen; **154&155B** Franck Socha/ Bluegreen.

First published in Great Britain in 2006 by
PAVILION BOOKS

An imprint of Anova Books Company Ltd
151 Freston Road, London W10 6TH

© Anova Books Company Ltd, 2006
Text © Oliver Dewar, 2006
Photography © see Picture Acknowledgements

Senior Editor: Emily Preece-Morrison
Design: www.pinkstripedesign.com
Jacket Design: Lotte Oldfield
Production: Oliver Jeffreys

A CIP catalogue record for this book is available
from the British Library.

ISBN 1 86205 728 1

Printed and bound in Wing King Tong Printers Company Ltd, China
Reproduction by Classicscan PTE Ltd, Singapore

10 9 8 7 6 5 4 3 2 1